ADVOCATING FOR CHILDREN LOOKED AFTER

This accessible guide provides a detailed and practical understanding of how to support Children Looked After (CLA), exploring concepts surrounding identity and the key role professionals can play by becoming advocates for these children. With a mixture of theory, reflection and application to practice, *Advocating for Children Looked After* considers contemporary topics, from adverse childhood experiences (ACEs), labelling and stigma, to the relationships surrounding Children Looked After.

Embedded within the chapters are positive everyday practices, case studies and dialogues, all of which help to create a safe space for children to develop their own sense of self. Throughout the book, outdated views are challenged and replaced with the voices of children and young people themselves, and strategies and opportunities are provided for the reader to truly understand the perspectives of Children Looked After and to develop their practice to best support their needs and well-being. Care is taken to refer to Children Looked After, rather than Looked After Children, placing the child at the forefront and before their care status.

Informative and reflective, this book offers both students and professionals a diverse insight into what makes a Child Looked After unique, with the aim of breaking the cycle in regard to their development and outcomes. It will be key reading for all professionals including those within education and social work, as well as those on undergraduate, postgraduate, and professional childhood courses.

Stella Smith is a senior lecturer and childhood placement lead at Nottingham Trent University, UK, and has worked in the Early Childhood sector for the last 10 years. She began her career as an Early Years teacher in private day nurseries then transitioning into further, then higher education. Stella is an adoptive mum and has developed a passion for promoting positive attachments for Children Looked After in Early Childhood Education and Care.

Kerry-Ann Rawson is a senior lecturer and course leader for the BA Childhood suite of programmes at Nottingham Trent University, UK. She started her teaching career in further education over 16 years ago where her role included teaching Early Education and Childhood studies programmes across all levels of learning as well as teaching Year 10 and 11 in a range of secondary schools. Kerry-Ann's upbringing has influenced her passion for developing positive practices for Children Looked After.

ADVOCATING FOR CHILDREN LOOKED AFTER

Promoting Positive Identities in Professional Practice

Stella Smith and Kerry-Ann Rawson

LONDON AND NEW YORK

Designed cover image: Getty Images

First published 2025
by Routledge
4 Park Square, Milton Park, Abingdon, Oxon OX14 4RN

and by Routledge
605 Third Avenue, New York, NY 10158

Routledge is an imprint of the Taylor & Francis Group, an informa business

© 2025 Stella Smith and Kerry-Ann Rawson

The right of Stella Smith and Kerry-Ann Rawson to be identified as authors of this work has been asserted in accordance with sections 77 and 78 of the Copyright, Designs and Patents Act 1988.

All rights reserved. No part of this book may be reprinted or reproduced or utilised in any form or by any electronic, mechanical, or other means, now known or hereafter invented, including photocopying and recording, or in any information storage or retrieval system, without permission in writing from the publishers.

Trademark notice: Product or corporate names may be trademarks or registered trademarks, and are used only for identification and explanation without intent to infringe.

British Library Cataloguing-in-Publication Data
A catalogue record for this book is available from the British Library

ISBN: 978-1-032-71082-2 (hbk)
ISBN: 978-1-032-71081-5 (pbk)
ISBN: 978-1-032-71697-8 (ebk)

DOI: 10.4324/9781032716978

Typeset in Interstate
by Deanta Global Publishing Services, Chennai, India

CONTENTS

Preface vi
Acknowledgements viii

1. Who Am I? 1
2. Stigmas and Labels 15
3. Adverse Childhood Experiences 28
4. Trauma and Neurodiversity 43
5. Attachments and Relationships 57
6. Who Are My Family and What Do They Do? 74
7. Government Agenda 89
8. Everyday superheroes 103
9. Teacher or Facilitator 115
10. Change in vision 129

Index 139

PREFACE

Advocating for Children Looked After: Promoting Positive Identities in Professional Practice came from our shared lived experiences but also as a result of engaging with a variety of professionals actively working with Children Looked After. We felt that despite many professionals doing a fantastic job of working with Children Looked After (CLA), they expressed a need for current and reflective materials to help them better navigate the complexities of CLA's identity. With this in mind, we wanted to write this book advocating for the child, to help professionals better understand who they are and where they have come from, as well as gain some further insight into why they are who they are. When supporting CLA, the individual must be the priority and the centre of all practice, therefore this book offers practical strategies and recommendations that we feel are vital to the overall well-being and achievement of CLA.

We hope that this book will empower professionals supporting CLA to really value the child and their experiences as well as understand the importance of the child's individual identity and the impact of their life story. We encourage professionals to use this book as a tool for true reflection on their practice and to approach their current knowledge and understanding through the eyes of the child.

Structure of the book

Throughout this book, we refer to all children in foster care, adoption, kinship, and residential placements as being "in care" and "looked after". Even though, in some legislative documents, the term Looked After Children (LAC) is used to describe children who are in care. We feel this term is dehumanising and children have questioned whether it means they are 'lacking in some way'. Throughout this book, we use the acronym CLA to refer to Children Looked After as this places the child before their care status.

The subject of this book is the range of identities of CLA and the economic, educational and societal impacts on their identity, self-perception and life outcomes, as seen through the lens of the children. This book has been written for students, practitioners and professionals who work alongside CLA and offers a child's perspective on the impact these adults have on the children's identity. This offers professionals a diverse insight into what makes a CLA unique, through the application of theory, reflection and practice to be able to break the cycle of CLA outcomes and development.

Chapters cover key concepts of children's identity and the role played by the economy, education and society in developing the self-perception of a CLA. Embedded throughout are contemporary topics such as adverse childhood experiences (ACEs), labelling and stigmas, as well as relationships surrounding CLA and how they are supported by governing bodies. Positive promotion of everyday practices and creating a safe space for CLA are woven into this book's dialogue. Throughout this journey, views will be challenged, positive practice will be celebrated, including the voice of children and young people, and current research is reviewed to provide a better understanding and awareness of CLA and their well-being.

The chapters are accessible and relatable to a range of practices and professions with consideration for the realities and challenges of working alongside CLA. The structure remains the same for each chapter, for ease of reading and returning to chapters. The book provides strategies and opportunities for the reader to reflect and engage with activities in relation to case studies as well as their individual practice.

ACKNOWLEDGEMENTS

As joint authors, we would both like to thank our colleagues who have motivated and encouraged us to put our pens to paper and share our strongly felt views with like-minded professionals. We would like to thank Aaron Bradbury for allowing us time and space to write while being a critical friend without whom this book would never have made it into print.

Individually, Stella would like to thank her daughter Kaylinn, who has been her motivation and driving force for improving the quality of care and support for Children Looked After. A massive thank you goes to her family and close friends for pushing her beyond her expectations of herself and having faith in her when she lacked faith in herself.

Kerry-Ann would like to thank her husband Simon and son Bailey for helping her prove to herself that a child raised in adversity can be as successful as any other child. They have helped her overcome statistics on Children Looked After. She is also grateful for all the everyday superheroes who have appeared throughout her life, who probably did not know how much they impacted and encouraged her to realise her potential.

1
Who Am I?

CHAPTER AIMS

This chapter will explore personal identity of Children Looked After (CLA) and what it means to be a Child in Care. By the end of this chapter, you will be able to do the following:

- Understand key terminology used when supporting Children Looked After and Children in Care.
- Explore children's individual backgrounds and the reasons for children becoming looked after.
- Reflect on the significance of children's individual identity and the impact this may have on children's behaviour.
- Develop an awareness of the needs of Children Looked After by the professionals caring for them.

Keywords

adoption, behaviour, Children Looked After, fostering, identity

Introduction

This chapter will explore the individual circumstances of children who are looked after by the state care system. We will review the different terminology used to describe children and the impact that the terminology used by professionals has on children with care experiences. This chapter attempts to understand the needs of different children from different backgrounds and situations. It is important to acknowledge early on in this book that no two children are the same. Two children may have the same parents and experiences going into care, but this does not mean that the children will have the same understanding and individual perceptions of the situation they are in.

Who Am I?

Currently there is some controversy over the correct terminology to use when referring to children who currently are or have experiences of being in care. In this section we will review the common definitions referring to children who are or have been in care and attempt to explain why there is controversy and what this means for children.

The NSPCC (2024) states that "a child who has been in care of their local authority for more than 24 hours is known as a looked after child". It is common among government policy and documentation for children to be referred to as "Looked After Children" and this is often abbreviated to LAC. The NSPCC (2024) also states that looked after children are also often referred to as Children in Care (CIC) and, more recently, Children Looked After (CLA) has been deemed the most appropriate terminology to use when discussing children being looked after by the local authority. To define a child looked after further, the NSPCC (2024) and the Welsh Government (2021) suggest that a child may be identified as in care when they have been placed into emergency care, following a carer being taken ill or arrested. It could also mean that a child is removed from their family home by social services or the police, as well as children in foster care and children living with potential adoptive parents. In Northern Ireland, this is a commonly accepted definition, however, it is extended to children who have left their family home for other reasons such as disability or illness of the child or a child being removed due to abuse, neglect or domestic violence (Northern Ireland, Department for Health 2022). The Scottish Government (2022) refers to Children Looked After as those who are looked after by a "corporate parent", suggesting that it is not just the local authority caring for children but anyone who earns money from caring for the child. This could be children in residential care, children cared for by kinship carers, adopted children, and those who have left care. Already you can see that there is some controversy between the status of a Child Looked After between the four nations of the United Kingdom.

For the purposes of this book, we have chosen to apply the terminology of Child/ren Looked After (CLA), however, this will still relate to all children considered to be in the care of local authorities, regardless of the reason. The reasoning behind this is because there are lots of criticisms of the term "Looked After Children" as, despite this being the most common reference to children in care, many professionals disagree with the "Looked After" label being before the child (Scottish Independent Care Review 2020). While completing the Scottish Independent Care Review (2020) many children felt that the acronym LAC had connotations of "lacking" in some way, whether it be lacking in family, development areas, or even love and support, which worsened children's already potentially low self-esteem and made them feel stigmatised (NSPCC 2024), which is reviewed in more detail in Chapter 2.

Why Am I "Looked After"?

In March 2023, 83,840 children in England were registered as being in the care of the local authority, according to the Office of National Statistics (2024). In this same year, 33,000 children started to be looked after and 31,680 children ceased to be looked after which is a 5–6 per cent increase from the previous year (2022). According to the Children Act 1989

(Children Act 1989), a child is looked after by the local authority if they fall into one of the following categories:

- The child is provided with accommodation for a period of more than 24 hours.
- The child is subject to a care order.
- The child is subject to a placement order.

A care order is an order issued by the courts which gives the local authority parental responsibility of a child, which allows the child to be taken into care (Children Act 1989). Children who have been issued a care order will have their parental responsibility shared with the local authority, however, the local authority will have the final say on the decisions regarding a child's life while they are in care (Children Act 1989). A care order can last until a child is 18 years old or a court deems the child can go back to live with their parents or a suitable guardian.

A placement order is also an order issued by the courts, however, this is done when the local authority believe that the child should be adopted (Adoption and Children Act 2002). Once the local authority receives a placement order for a child, a suitable adoptive family can be sought for the child. When a child is given a placement order, it means that the child will not be returning to their previous caregivers and parental responsibility will be transferred to the child's adoptive parents (Adoption and Children Act 2002).

There are many reasons why a child may be taken into care but Figure 1.1 presents some of the most common ones.

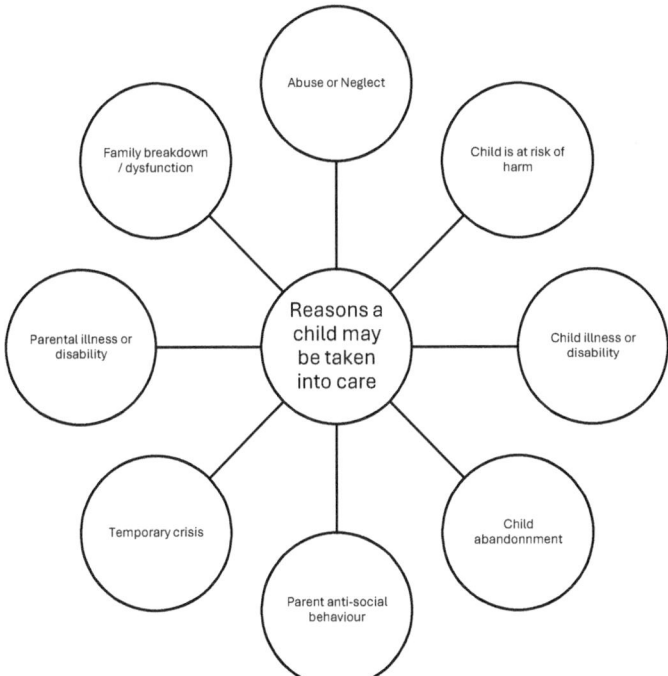

Figure 1.1 Possible reasons for being in care

According to the Office of National Statistics (2024), in 2023, of the 83,840 children in the care of the local authority:

- 54,810 children (65 per cent) were taken into care as a result of or being at risk of abuse or neglect;
- 10,570 (13 per cent) due to family breakdown or dysfunction;
- 7,290 (9 per cent) lack of parenting or abandonment;
- 6,160 (7 per cent) families were going through a temporary crisis and unable to meet their child's needs;
- 4,010 (5 per cent) due to the child's or parent's illness or disability;
- 1,000 (1 per cent) due to low income or socially unacceptable behaviour.

Here are some case studies to serve as examples of why children may be in care.

CASE STUDY 1.1

Child in care following abuse identified in the Children Act (1989/2004) Section 31 (9)

Daisy is 4 years old and attends nursery three times a week. Practitioners in the setting have noticed that Daisy, after having four days off from nursery, returns with several small bruises to the tops of her arms and legs. Practitioners have questioned her mum regarding these bruises and mum explains that Daisy is clumsy and falls over her toys a lot. The setting has referred this to the Designated Safeguarding Lead (DSL) and escalated to the Local Authority Designated Officer (LADO). Today Daisy informed her key person that her mum has made the bruises, and she shows them a bruise on the back of her neck where she tells the key person that mum had carried her up the stairs and locked her in her room. After referring this to the LADO, Daisy was collected from nursery and placed into foster care pending investigation into her mum.

CASE STUDY 1.2

Child in care following the likelihood of experiencing significant harm identified in the Children Act (1989) Section 31 (2)

Joshua is 10 years old and lives at home with his parents and two younger siblings. Each night when Joshua is in bed, he can hear his parents fighting and arguing downstairs. Sometimes the shouting gets so loud that the neighbours bang on the door to tell his parents to be quiet, one time he even heard the police come to find out what was happening. This morning when Joshua woke up, he noticed that his mum had a cut under her eye. Joshua's mum told him that she had walked into the top kitchen cupboard. Because of this, Joshua does not sleep well, he is worried about his mum.

At school his teacher notices that he does not pay attention in lessons. The teacher asks him what has been happening and Joshua tells him what is happening at home. The teacher refers this to the DSL and the LADO. Joshua is collected from school by a designated social worker.

CASE STUDY 1.3

Child removed from the family home under the Emergency Protection Order of the Children Act (1989) Section 44

Kacey lives with her parents and young sibling. Her house is a loud house and there is often lots of banging. The neighbours always complain to the police that their house is too noisy, and they always knock the door to shout at her parents. This time the shouting got bad. Kacey's little brother was screaming really loudly and mummy's friend who had been staying with them in the living room kept trying to leave but Kacey's dad would not let her out of the front door. This time the police came and pushed past Kacey's dad and came into the house, there were three of them. Mummy's friend was upset and had hurt herself; Kacey and her brother were hiding. The police arrested Kacey's mum and dad and a police officer put Kacey and her brother into a police car and took them away.

Reflective Questions

Case Study 1.1 Daisy

1. If you were Daisy's key person, would you have reported this incident to the DSL and LADO?
2. Would you have expected the result to be that Daisy would be in care?
3. Knowing this, would you still have made the referral to the LADO?

Case Study1.2 Joshua

1. If you were Joshua's teacher, would you have reported this incident to the DSL and LADO?
2. What reasons do you feel could have resulted Joshua being placed into care rather than returning home to his mum?

Case Study 1.3 Kacey

1. Why do you think the police forced their way into the house this time? What do you think they saw to make them do this?
2. Do you think Kacey recognises or understands what has happened in her family home?

My Identity

Identity, by definition, is the "fact of being who or what a person or thing is" (*Cambridge English Dictionary* 2024). What this means for children and adults alike is that their identity consists of the characteristics that make up who they are as a person. A child's identity is influenced and formed through their social interactions, family, culture, community, and their lived experiences (Crowley 2017). Children try to gain a sense of self and identity when they associate with other people around them, but also observe and witness behaviour of others and imitate these in different social situations. Therefore, they are developing not only an individual identity for themselves but also a social identity, a persona of who they are when they are interacting with other people.

Article 8 of the United Nations Conventions of the Rights of the Child (UN 1989) states that all children have the right to an identity, children must have an official record of who they are. Article 7 also supports that all children have the right to a name that is officially recognised by the government and the right to a nationality, to belong to a country. As Crowley (2017) mentions, children's identity goes beyond a name and a record of nationality but also the right to culture, language, and religion.

The next few sections of this chapter will summarise different theoretical perspectives surrounding CLA's identity and offer possible interpretations to how their identity has been formed and shaped.

Identity Theory

Identity theory focuses on the relationship between the mind and body and asserts that the mind and body are two different expressions of one material reality. Identity theory was introduced almost 30 years ago and seeks to understand the identity of individuals from a sociological perspective, exploring the sources of human interactions and society and the consequences that society and its interactions have on a person's individual identity and perception of themselves. According to Davidson and Fouts (2024), identity encompasses the values people hold and in turn dictates the choices that they make.

Erikson's Psychosocial Theory

With this in mind, the work of Erik Erikson helps to explain how children's culture, background, and lived experiences shape children's individual identities. Erikson's eight psychosocial stages explain how children's lived experiences are necessary to children's development and understanding of themselves (Marcia 2020). In Table 1.1 you can see how Erikson explained the experience that a child had in relation to their particular stage of life and what this means for CLA.

Erikson believed that children create identities for themselves to reflect the situations they find themselves in so that they are able to survive. As can be seen in the eight stages, if CLA are not given the positive role models to shape their identity, this could have a lasting impact throughout their lives. This links to Reay (2021) who explores the idea of fluid identity, meaning a child's identity does not have to be fixed and it can be adapted to

Table 1.1 Erikson's eight stages of psychosocial theory

Stage	Basic conflict	Description	What this could mean for CLA
Infancy Birth to 1 year	Trust vs Mistrust	The child will trust their basic needs will be met	Children mistrust that their needs are being met so adapt to ensure they are able to survive
Early Childhood 1-3 years	Autonomy vs Shame	Children are able to develop a sense of independence in many tasks	Children feel shame and embarrassment at not being able to do tasks independently through having a lack of support
Play Age 3-6 years	Initiative vs Guilt	Children are able to take initiative on some activities	The child will feel guilt at if unsuccessful in activities and cross boundaries as a result
School Age 7-11 years	Industry vs Inferiority	Children develop self-confidence in their ability and competency	Children develop a sense of inferiority if not equal to their peers
Adolescence 12-18 years	Identity vs Confusion	Children develop their own identity and roles in society	Children will confuse their role and change identity to reflect their confusion
Early Adulthood 19-29 years	Intimacy vs Isolation	Establish secure and intimate relationships with others	Struggle to form and maintain relationships, feel isolated with no secure sense of belonging
Middle Ages 30-64 years	Generativity vs Stagnation	Form a family and contribute to society	May find family life and structure difficult to maintain, finding connections within the community may be a struggle
Old Age	Integrity vs Despair	Assess and make sense of life	Feelings of loss and despair at lack of clear identity and sense of self

different situations and environments. For CLA, as for all other children, their identities will be shaped by their lived experiences. Therefore, where a child has experienced a volatile family home, they will learn to adapt and shape themselves, learning from the situation. Children will learn how to present themselves to different professionals so that it is believed that the child responds to certain situations and people in the ways they have displayed.

> Reflective Questions
>
> 1. How could Erikson's psychosocial stages be used to support the identity formation of CLA?
> 2. What could professionals do to help CLA associate with the positive conflicts in Erikson's psychosocial stages?

Erikson's psychosocial theory poses some key issues for CLA, mainly that of the child recognising themselves as the labels given to them by professionals in specific situations, or they will identify as the child from a specific upbringing or lived experience (Marcia 2020). Both identities have a detrimental impact on children's well-being as they journey through life. This topic is explored in further detail in Chapter 2. The next key theory of importance for children's identity is that of Pierre Bourdieu.

Bourdieu: Identity Movements in Field, Cultural Capital, and Habitus

Pierre Bourdieu associates a child's identity with the lived environment and relationships that a child has experienced (Carter and Crawford 2020). Bourdieu identifies these as different fields of childhood; each field is a different environment or different relationship being experienced. He states that a child's identity is not defined by their social status but the quality of relationships that a child has with those around them. Children's individual identity is shaped through the practices of childhood, their experiences of different relationships, and the hierarchy within those relationships (Brown 2022). This refers to Bourdieu's cultural capital, with children being able to reflect relationships and situations they have an understanding of. For a CLA who has experienced trauma, abuse, or neglect in their family home, their identity may be that of a child who must appease the adults to be able to survive and thrive. Bourdieu suggests that children are conditioned to identify in their social situations. However, children who have experienced similar social situations are not always inclined to have similar identities. This goes back to the opening of the chapter where it was noted that despite two children experiencing the same background and circumstances, they may have completely different perspectives of themselves and outlook on the world around them (Brock 2023). This relates to the child's habitus, with children being around others with similar experiences, although they may not have the same identity, there is a harmonised sense of belonging from shared understanding. Bourdieu argues that, for CLA, certain feelings, opinions, and social interactions or behaviours can be reflective of the world around them and therefore their sense of identity and personality in different situations becomes second nature but is reflective of how they have interpreted their childhood experiences (Brock 2023).

> *Reflective Questions*
>
> 1. *In your opinion, do you think CLA can form multiple identities in order to manage and cope with different social interactions and environments?*
> 2. *As professionals, how do we distinguish between children's different identities?*

Bauman's Notion of Liquidity Modernity

Zygmunt Bauman (2004) explored children's sense of belonging in the community as part of their identity, explaining that children are constantly searching for their identity to explore who they are versus what the community and society expects them to be. Liquid modernity explored the concept that children actively negotiate their own identity as a result of situations and circumstances out of their control (Best 2016). For CLA, this may mean they are required to present different identities and personalities for different situations and circumstances to help them survive as best as possible. For Bauman (2011), the fact that children live in fear, uncertainty, and instability prevents CLA building a consistent identity due to the unpredictability of their lifestyle and home life. Children who have a sense of belonging and a strong identity can be seen as having solid modernity, they have confidence in who they are and where they come from. For CLA, liquid modernity affects those who do not have a secure sense of belonging; like a liquid, they slide between gaps and spaces and adapt to the situations and circumstances surrounding them. Best (2016) states that children who have liquid modernity can be seen as "not normal" or "not ordinary", which immediately implies that there is something wrong or at fault with CLA. Bauman et al. (2015) state we are in an era of solid modernity, meaning that society is made for people who belong, and those who do not have solid modernity are often excluded. This can be the case for many CLA who often, through no fault of their own, have no choice but to blend into different situations, taking on the persona of a chameleon, adapting, and blending into the background of the situation they are in. Bauman and Raud (2015) argue that this a well-developed coping strategy for CLA and this is their way of managing society and social situations in the best way they can. However, for Bauman (2011), the concept of CLA "not being normal" can impact their own perceptions of themselves negatively as well as heightening their feelings of exclusion on not fitting in.

> Reflective Questions
>
> 1. Is Bauman's liquid modernity different to Bourdieu's identity of movements?
> 2. Why is it important for children to manage society and situational environments?
> 3. How do you think this makes children feel, having to change and adapt their identity to navigate society?

Eaude: Culture and Identity

Tony Eaude (2019) explores the concept that identity is a constantly changing narrative based on how a child sees themselves and how they are perceived by others. All children have multiple and overlapping identities which represent the norms, values, and beliefs that a child holds as developed from their experiences of socialisation, gender, race, religion, and cultural background. Eaude (2019) firmly believes, similar to Bauman et al. (2015), that identities are fluid and changing rather than fixed. Eaude differs from Bauman, suggesting that this fluidity is normal for all children, not just those who have experienced adversity, but is adopted from an early age which encapsulates a set of broadly shared beliefs and practices which are developed and built over time. As a child changes and experiences new cultures, their identity and sense of self also change and develop. Eaude also states that children's identities are constructed around primary and secondary socialisation where the influence on the child is primarily in the home. Children who are not care experienced find their home environment will help them develop strong and secure beliefs and sense of self. For CLA, who may not have experienced a secure and loving culture, their beliefs and sense of self are likely to be representative of what they have witnessed. For example, a child who has experienced feelings of unworthiness or been devalued will hold that identity close with them as they grow. For a child to grow positively and maintain a positive identity and self-perception, there is a need for trusting relationships, warm emotional environments, and adults who advocate and guide children, which helps children to gradually become older and more confident in their sense of self and ability to make positive choices for themselves. However, as discussed earlier in this chapter, it is unlikely that CLA will always have experienced these warm emotional environments and trusting relationships that Eaude (2019) describes. Therefore CLA's sense of self is less firmly rooted, and a child is more likely to develop situational identity to help navigate the world around them with less of a hold on solid beliefs and values.

> *Reflective Questions*
>
> 1. In your opinion, do you think children will even understand their true identity if they continue to have overlapped and multiple identities?
> 2. Is it important for children to have one solid identity or is it acceptable to have multiple identities?
> 3. What impact could multiple identities have on children as they grow into adulthood?

CASE STUDIES REVISITED

With these theories in mind, there could be a potential negative impact on CLA's identity and how they perceive themselves in different situations. Let's go back to our original three case studies and see how their identity may have been shaped as a result of their experiences.

CASE STUDY 1.1: DAISY

Daisy has always been open and talkative with her friends and practitioners in her nursery setting. Since being in foster care Daisy has become withdrawn from her key person, she is quiet and calm around adults. With her friends, Daisy does not stand out from the crowd, she watches lots of play and mimics the play of the other children, but she will only join in when the children around her invite her to participate.

CASE STUDY 1.2: JOSHUA

Joshua has begun to demonstrate anger and frustration towards his peers and the adults around him. He actively seeks out situations which are not appropriate and risky but is unable to express why he does this. His peer group changes on a regular basis as he gets into trouble with the teachers in his school and other children shy away from him, other than a select few boys who gravitate towards Joshua.

CASE STUDY 1.3: KACEY

Kacey has developed a nervousness and anxiety at loud noises and sharp movements since the incident with the police. When Kacey is uncomfortable or senses danger, she will run and remove herself from the situation. When she is with her brother, Kacey is playful and boisterous but with others she is timid and reluctant to engage with children or adults

CLA have experienced at least one, if not multiple significant, harmful or risky events for them to be in the care of the local authority, which is explored in more detail in Chapter 3. These will have an impact on how they see those around them and how they respond to different professionals, practitioners, and peers. This can be explored in more depth in Chapter 6, as well as Chapter 8 and Chapter 9. However, behaviour changes such as those portrayed in the case studies are common for CLA as they have adapted their behaviour and responses to things and people they perceive to be a threat. The most common behaviour responses CLA display are flight, fight, or freeze responses in order to protect themselves of potential threats they may face. This behaviour response is detailed in Chapter 3.

Reflective Questions

1. *Do you think the behaviour changes of the three children in the case studies are a direct result of their experience of being in care?*
2. *Do you feel this behaviour forms part of their identity?*
3. *Will their behaviour impact on how society, professionals, and practitioners view the child and form opinions of them?*

What Do I Need?

What is clear from all of the identified theoretical perspectives summarised in this chapter, is that children need a strong sense of self to help them navigate their journey in life. Part

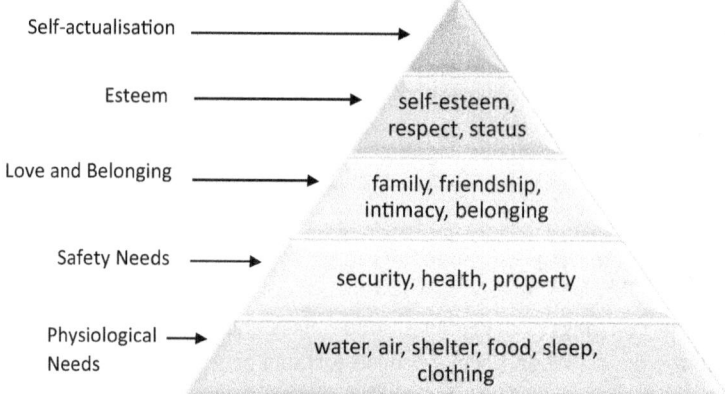

Figure 1.2 Maslow's Hierarchy of Needs

of that strong sense of self comes from having a safe and secure environment. This can be likened to Maslow's Hierarchy of Needs (Figure 1.2).

Physiological and safety needs are the foundation of a child's life. As identified early in this chapter, the majority of CLA are in the care of the local authority because these basic needs have not been met by their primary care givers. Already, CLA have not had those secure foundations and therefore this makes it difficult to meet their self-actualisation identified at the top of the pyramid. By being placed in care, foster families, carers, or guardians, under supervision of the local authority, are able to meet the safety and physiological needs of the children which hopefully begins to repair the damage made by early adverse experiences. This will be discussed in more detail in Chapter 3. Next, it is important for the adults caring for CLAs to ensure they have love and belonging, according to Maslow (1943) and all the other theorists explored in this chapter, children need advocates, adults who are on their side to provide them with love, care, and affection, who will help them develop their own sense of self and feel they belong. This will be explored further in Chapter 5.

Naish (2018) identifies that children in care need a strong "unassailable safe base". By this, she means that adults and carers for CLA need to provide children with a warm, nurturing and approachable environment for them to truly be themselves and explore who they are in the world they have found themselves in. Naish states, in order for children to fully be themselves, the adults in their lives need to provide consistency which children can rely on which can encompass both routine and firm boundaries but also being honest, reliable, and emotionally available to the children, allowing them to feel they are there with them, helping them to construct their sense of belonging and in turn develop their identity. This concept is present throughout this book and we explore a range of different possible strategies for supporting children's development of love and belonging which will naturally lead to the building of their esteem and sense of self and self-actualisation.

Summary

In this chapter we have explored the individual circumstances of CLA and the role their individual circumstances plays in the development of their individual identity. Key terminology has been reviewed for the significance of this and the impact it has on children. Language and terminology are explored further in Chapter 2 where you will find lots of examples of the impact that different language and labels has on CLA. We have identified different theoretical perspectives surrounding CLA's identity and the impact this can have on children's identity and sense of self-development. Understanding children's circumstances and backgrounds further can be explored in Chapter 3 and a review of strategies for supporting children's individual needs can be found in Chapter 5.

References

Adoption and Children Act 2002. Available at: https://www.legislation.gov.uk/ukpga/2002/38/notes/division/2.3

Bauman, Z. (2004). *Wasted Lives: Modernity and Its Outcasts*. Cambridge: Polity.

Bauman, Z. (2008). *The Art of Life*. Cambridge: Polity.

Bauman, Z. (2011). A Natural History of Evil. In Z. Bauman (ed.), *Collateral Damage: Social Inequalities in a Global Age*. Cambridge: Polity, pp. 128-149.

Bauman, Z., Bauman, I., and Kociatkiewicz, J. (2015). *Management in a Liquid Modern World*. Cambridge: Polity.

Bauman, Z. and Raud, R. (2015). *Practices of Selfhood*. Cambridge: Polity.

Best, S. (2016). Zygmunt Bauman: On What It Means to Be Included. *Power and Education*, 8(2), 124-139. DOI: 10.1177/1757743816649197

Brock, T. (2023). *Welcome to Social Theory*. London: SAGE Publications

Brown, A. (2022). Identities In and Around Organizations: Towards an Identity Work Perspective. *Human Relations*, 75(7), 1205-1237. DOI: 10.1177/0018726721993910

Cambridge English Dictionary (2024). Identity. Available at: https://dictionary.cambridge.org/dictionary/english/identity

Carter, C. and Crawford, S. (2020). Bourdieu and Identity: Class, History and Field Structure. In A.D. Brown (ed.), *The Oxford Handbook of Identities in Organizations*. Oxford: Oxford University Press. https://doi.org/10.1093/oxfordhb/9780198827115.013.9

Children Act 1989 (c.31 and 44). Available at: https://www.legislation.gov.uk/ukpga/1989/41/contents

Crowley, K. (2017). *Child Development*. 2nd edn. London: Sage.

Davidson, K. and Fouts, H.N. (2024). Fostering Children's Racialized Identities in Early Childhood Education. *Early Years*, 44(2), 251-266.

Eaude, T. (2019). The Role of Culture and Traditions in How Young Children's Identities Are Constructed. *International Journal of Children's Spirituality*, 24(1), 5-19. DOI: 10.1080/1364436X.2019.1619534

Marcia, J.E. (2020). Psychosocial Stages of Development (Erikson). In V. Zeigler-Hill and T.K. Shackelford (eds), *Encyclopedia of Personality and Individual Differences*. Cham: Springer. DOI: 10.1007/978-3-319-24612-3_1418

Maslow, A.H. (1943). A Theory of Human Motivation. *Psychological Review*, 50, 370-396.

Naish, S. (2018). *The A-Z of Therapeutic Parenting: Strategies and Solutions*. London: Jessica Kingsley Publishers.

Northern Ireland, Department for Health. (2022). Looked after Children. Available at: https://www.health-ni.gov.uk/articles/looked-after-children

NSPCC (National Society for the Prevention of Cruelty to Children). (2024). Looked After Children. Available at: https://learning.nspcc.org.uk/children-and-families-at-risk/looked-after-children

Office of National Statistics. (2024). Children Looked After in England Including Adoptions. Available at: https://explore-education-statistics.service.gov.uk/find-statistics/children-looked-after-in-england-including-adoptions

Reay, D. (2021). The Working Classes and Higher Education: Meritocratic Fallacies of Upward Mobility in the United Kingdom. *European Journal of Education*, 56(1), 53-64. DOI: 10.1111/ejed.12438.

Scottish Government. (2022). Looked After Children. Available at: https://www.gov.scot/policies/looked-after-children/

Scottish Independent Care Review. (2020). Available at: scvo.scot/research/evidence-library/independent...

UN. (1989). Convention on the Rights of the Child. United Nations General Assembly. Available at: https://www.unicef.org/child-rights-convention

Welsh Government. (2021). Review of Adverse Childhood Experiences (ACE) Policy: Report. Available at: https://gov.wales/review-adverse-childhood-experiences-ace-policy-report-html

2
Stigmas and Labels

> **CHAPTER AIMS**
>
> This chapter will explore the impact of stigma and labels on Children Looked After (CLA) and their identity. By the end of this chapter, you will be able to do the following:
>
> - Examine how the labels given to CLA can adversely affect the formation of their identity.
> - Explore the impact of labels with links made to the concept of stigma.
> - Question the role of language used within the professional sector when referring to and talking to CLA.
> - Consider why language matters when working with CLA or care experienced.
>
> **Keywords**
>
> identity, injustice, labelling, marginalisation, motivation, self-fulfilling prophecy, stigmatisation

Introduction

There is no doubt that labels and the stigma associated with them are prevalent in our society. However, it is difficult to imagine how these can affect a child's identity, particularly if you have not faced these situations as a child yourself. It is possible that in your professional training, you have been taught about the connotations associated with the use of labels in your field. In this chapter we will discuss how this may differ for CLA or children who have been in care. Since language is so ingrained and habitual in our culture, we may be unable to recognise that the words and phrases we employ can cause hurt and harm to others, to the point where we need to explore how desensitised we have become. We will consider why language matters when working with CLA.

Terminology

Historically, in the United Kingdom, the term "Looked After Children" (LAC) has been used by the legislation, in policy and in the literature to describe children who are cared for away from home and they are commonly referred to as LAC or care-experienced children (Horsburgh 2022). The National Society for the Prevention of Cruelty to Children (NSPCC) continues to use these terms in some of its publications (NSPCC 2023; 2024). In contrast, in England, the term Looked After Children (LAC) is being replaced with the term Children Looked After (CLA). The Department for Education (DfE 2022) uses this term in recent reports and policies and Ofsted uses the terms "care leavers" or "children in care" in their published reports. In the evolution of any language, it takes time for it to become fully integrated into the linguistic fabric of our society, and at the moment, it almost seems that different influential parties each are bidding for their own terminology.

Nonetheless, it does not matter which terminology is used but what they are referring to. Ultimately, all of these aforementioned terms categorise fairly generally that the child has not been well cared for at some point in their lives and ultimately carry with them presumptions about the type of support to be provided to these children, as well as how society will view them. A child in care is at risk of discrimination for the simple reason that they are in care (Fieller and Loughlin 2022). The majority of professionals and practitioners working within the care system want to improve the lives of the children they work alongside but are finding themselves facing challenges when doing so. Horsburgh (2022) argues that tension arises because those working in education, welfare and the care services are reluctant to stigmatise CLA by labelling them with these terms but find themselves having to do so. This is because they must label and allocate children to certain groups so support services are assigned to them. In order to categorise children into groups in need of the appropriate support, labels are required. Having knowledge and an understanding of how labels are used to stigmatise groups in our society, professionals are faced with the dilemma of using labels for the children they work with. It is claimed by Fieller and Loughlin (2022) that the terminology we use when talking about CLA damages our preconceptions and reinforces them as they continue to be used. Ultimately, we need to continue to use labels so children are supported, even when these labels are in the process of changing in our society. As a result of being looked after, children often face obstacles in their daily lives, such as the breakdown of primary attachments (Cocker and Allain 2012) and the experience of loss, and subsequently being categorised and labelled is an unwelcome complication.

There is no denying that humans are inherently social creatures, as we must have social connections and relationships to feel connected to each other. As a result of these connections, we can create stronger bonds between us, as well as create divisions between those in our group and those who are not members of our group. Fitting in with peer groups is one of the most important issues for all young people, and CLA might not wish to share too much information about their family circumstances or the fact that they are looked after. Developing peer relationships can be very challenging when a child is in care, especially if they have frequently moved because of the location of their placements. This may mean that CLA have attended many schools and have been unable to build bonds with their peers. The first impression that a child makes when they start a new school is very important, and

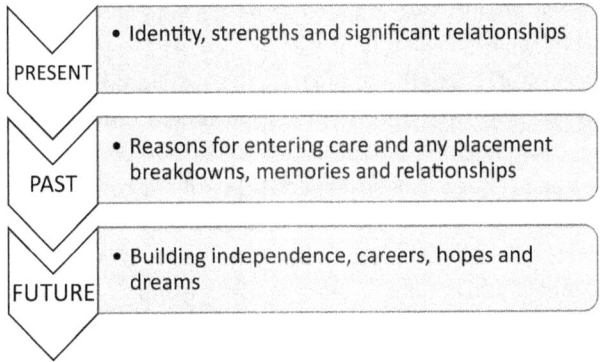

Figure 2.1 Overview of what needs to be included in life story work

Source: adapted from NICE (2021).

they are probably not going to want their new classmates to know about their looked-after status when they start a new school. CLA will undoubtedly be familiar with the stigma associated with their situation, along with the preconceptions that come with it and will already have faced the challenge of dealing with the different ways in which others treat them due to their situation. There is growing evidence that stigma is internalised by children, as reported by Dansey, Shbero and John (2019). CLA believe that their care status will lead to bullying, so they choose to keep it a secret as a consequence. Even though many of them may not wish to carry over the stigma to their new school, it is important to keep in mind that the professionals within the setting can easily imply to their peers that these children are looked after.

When working with CLA, discretion is essential, especially when using terminology such as that outlined above. One way to help support CLA and the development of their identity is through life story work. Life story work is an intervention that aims to help children and young people understand and accept their personal history as well as help them to make sense of their journey in care and their identity (NICE 2021). In accordance with legislation, such as the Children and Families Act 2014, local authorities are required to assist CLA in documenting their past to avoid confusion regarding their identity. As soon as children are placed in care, social workers are expected to develop their life stories and devote time to aspects of the present, past, and future tailored to the needs of each child (Figure 2.1). It is worth noting that life story work has not been without its critics, with many adoptive parents expressing concerns about poor quality, errors, and a lack of attention to content (Selwyn, Wijedasa and Meakings 2014). It is likely that inexperienced social workers who have been given this to do as part of their role may not have been provided with the training they need to be able to deal with these situations with the sensitivity and care they deserve.

Labelling

Our identity is defined by the relationship between how we perceive ourselves and how others perceive and react to us. In other words, our identity is constantly evolving rather than being static. We live in a society in which social rules and norms provide context for the development of our identity over time. Specifically, educational settings impose social rules that may indicate whether the school defines a child as conformist or non-conformist, successful or unsuccessful (Bartlett and Burton 2020). Children will often find themselves being labelled as conformists when they display behaviour, attitudes and academic achievement conducive to the dominant school values or as non-conformists when displaying behaviour, attitudes and academic achievement that are not considered part of the school values (Hargreaves 1967). In turn, this label can be associated with the child who may find themselves negatively defined by others and teachers. Day (2017) reported that children who are commonly labelled as naughty from an early age and singled out as being problematic feel an overwhelming lack of power and agency and are more likely to forge an identity for themselves with other children who have been similarly labelled. According to Bartlett and Burton (2020), labelling influences children's sense of themselves and their identity, thereby affecting their performance and potential to succeed. CLA need to be able to build positive relationships with those around them in order for them to feel valued, listened to and not feel stigmatised. If, however, CLA perceive that these adults already regard them as only a label, they are unlikely to be willing to foster and build relationships with them.

We need to understand the sociological concept of labelling theory to understand how labels can affect how we develop our identity and how it affects our sense of belonging. A major influence and development of the labelling theory is Becker (1973) through his book, *Outsiders: Studies in the Sociology of Deviance*, which he wrote to show that criminality was a personal decision of the individual and that deviance was a characteristic of human nature in general. However, his evidence led him to challenge this initial assumption and to state that the preconceptions we have of each other can influence behaviour. Thus, people can become victims if they are labelled as "deviant", which negatively impacts their identity and increases the likelihood of them committing acts deemed deviant (Brock 2023).

It is important to emphasise that children learn from the adults around them, and they are extremely adaptable when it comes to identifying the use of labels in the classroom, both for themselves and for others. The initial judgements made by teachers about children in their classes are often based on stereotyped practices from their previous teaching experience that they believe justify the attribution of a label. For instance, whether a child is well-behaved, naughty or clever will determine how that teacher will act and make classroom-based decisions. This label is then reinforced within the confines of the classroom if the warranted behaviour is repeated. A child may not be aware that a negative label has been assigned to them until after it has occurred. The role of labelling in schools, therefore, reinforces teachers' expectations of the children they teach which can have a serious effect on children's identity. The other concern regarding this issue is the fact that professionals need to examine the underlying causes of the problematic behaviour so they can determine which kind of support is most appropriate for the child, rather than simply labelling them. If underlying needs are identified and support is given, children are more likely to avoid being isolated and labelled based on their behaviour (Day 2017).

Mannay et al. (2017) in their research into the consequences of children being labelled "looked after" in school found that children and young people were actively aware of their "looked-after" status and that this label given by both their teachers and peers made them feel different. In this research, many of the CLA expressed frustration at being viewed and understood through the lens of being "looked after". It was noted that while these CLA had aspirations for the future, they were alert to the identity that society envisioned for them and found themselves constantly challenged by the assumptions associated with being "looked after". The results of this research, however, indicate that some CLA were supported and encouraged by their teachers in terms of their aspirations; however, most CLA confided that their teachers had low expectations regarding their academic ability or career trajectory. This supports the widely acknowledged notion that CLA have lower educational achievements compared to other children (DfE 2020). Academic achievements and outcomes will be discussed in more detail in Chapters 7 and 9.

> **CASE STUDY 2.1**
>
> Two children are talking and giggling in their class and are not listening or paying attention to the teacher. The teacher notices this unwanted behaviour and warns the children to be quiet. After a few minutes, the talking and giggling continue. The teacher removes one of the children from the class to "cool off" in the corridor.

Reflective Questions

1. The teacher has already labelled one child as naughty. Do you think this was the child that was removed?
2. Do you think this child may feel that they are being picked on and treated differently to others?

There are positive and negative connotations linked to the labels that we may be given, and we will respond to each very differently. Having a label, either positive or negative, has the power to change the behaviour of the children we work with, as it would change ours if we were given a label. Labelling theory suggests that the labels imposed on us affect our sense of self and our identity and, in turn, have the power to influence our performance and potential to achieve. Would you feel valued and highly thought of if you were labelled as being lazy? Would this label help you to perform well as expected? Try the activity in Table 2.1.

Table 2.1 Which are positive and which are negative?

Examples of labels	Positive	Negative
Loud		
Gifted		
Unfocused		
Talented		
Low ability		
Naughty		
Able		
Bright		
Dreamer		
Clever		
Lazy		

> **Reflective Questions**
>
> 1. Did you have a label?
> 2. Do labels have impact? Long-term, short-term?
> 3. Are labels passed through the family?
> 4. Do others treat us according to our label?
> 5. Can children break free from their label or is it easier for them to develop a self-image that matches their label?
> 6. What labels may a CLA have?
> 7. Is CLA a label? Is it positive or negative? Is this hurting the children we care for?

CASE STUDY 2.2 PART A

As a child who has experienced care throughout most of her childhood, Arla started to notice the labels she was given during her latter secondary school years both in conversation with teachers and also in her annual student reports.

In one of Arla's classes, the teacher was discussing the concept of resilience and how it refers to an individual being able to "bounce back" and function competently despite having experienced stressful and adverse situations. The teacher then turned to Arla in front of the class and exclaimed that Arla was the most resilient young person she had taught. The other students quickly looked at her, but nothing was said. Arla felt embarrassed at the attention but then started to become angry.

> **Reflective Question**
>
> 1. Why do you think Arla began to feel embarrassed and angry?

CASE STUDY 2.2 PART B

In Arla's life, she has experienced a lot of adverse and stressful situations, but she does not feel that she has "bounced back", as some may think. She does not understand how her teacher could presume to know that she has simply "bounced back" and carried on as if nothing had happened. Arla felt she had been unfairly labelled and then judged as being resilient for just being a child who has experienced care. She also lives in poverty where her mother spends a lot of their benefits on cigarettes and alcohol rather than on the basics such as food, toiletries and clothes. Arla is often bullied at school because of her hair which always looks straggly and limp because she very rarely washes it using shampoo but instead uses cheap washing-up liquid. Arla cannot understand how she can "bounce back" from that.

Reflective Question

1. Is Arla's anger justified?

CASE STUDY 2.2 PART C

Arla was given her annual student report and when she returned home after school, she read it to her mother. When reading this Arla fell across the phrase "factory material" and was unsure of what this meant. She had heard it many times growing up but did not know what it meant exactly. The next day, she spoke to her form room teacher and asked about this phrase. Arla's teacher responded that he did not like this particular term, however, he understood what the writer was trying to convey. He continued to inform her that this meant that in the context of the sentence she is a very able student who will excel as factory material, in other words, would be suited to working in a factory. This preconceived notion that she did not have any aspirations other than to work in a factory upset Arla as she felt it was based on her background and upbringing. Up until this point, Arla had started to like the idea of attending college after finishing her GCSEs. This idea soon faded, and Arla soon started to work in a toy manufacturing factory after leaving school.

> **Reflective Questions**
>
> 1. Do you think that Arla would have attended college if she had not received this report?
> 2. Do you think the teacher who wrote the report meant to come across as being negative or positive?
> 3. Do children like Arla develop a self-image that matches their label?

The concept of self-fulfilling prophecy is related to the labelling process and indicates how influential it can be in shaping behaviour. If a child is labelled as lazy and this has been reinforced, that child will learn to behave and live up to that label. Why should that child change their behaviour and appear less lazy when that label has been attached to them? The concept of a self-fulfilling prophecy was first coined by Merton (1948) through his work in social sciences, who claimed that in the beginning, the self-fulfilling prophecy is a false definition which evokes new behaviour which then makes the original false definition come true. In a nutshell, individuals change their behaviour to fit the definition. If a child was told repeatedly by their teacher that they were not clever, the child would start to perceive this to be true and behave in a way that fits the definition, including not trying their best in their academic efforts. The child would alter their behaviour to meet the expectations of this self-fulfilling prophecy. Why would they bother to even attempt to try harder in school? You may argue that a child's sense of will and personality would go against this prophecy. However, it is difficult to do this and forge their path when the false definition has been given by someone as influential as their teacher and other teachers in their school. As professionals working with CLA, we need to understand the importance and consequences of this particular social theory and to appreciate how impactful and influential we can be in a child's life with something as simple as how we perceive and define those CLA we work alongside.

How children learn to view themselves and how in control they feel are referred to as their "self-efficacy". Bandura (1997) introduced the concept of self-efficacy which he viewed as being pivotal in the way that children think and behave, as well as their emotional state. There are four key psychological processes which directly influence the self-efficacy beliefs we all hold: cognitive, motivational, affective and selection (Macblain, Dunn and Luke 2017) (Table 2.2).

All of us, children and adults, are motivated by different factors and why we choose to do something is affected by materialistic motivation, social motivation and intrinsic motivation (Stewart and Harris 2007). Intrinsic learners are able to take responsibility for their own learning and are problem-solvers, which means that they are more likely to evaluate their progress in order to improve their skills.

Stigmas and Labels 23

Table 2.2 Influences on self-efficacy beliefs

Influence	Definition
Cognitive	How children think plays an important role in how they behave and what drives their behaviour. Children are able to use their cognition to meet challenges
Motivational	Children apply themselves to manage challenges and keep trying to overcome them. Alternatively, children may lack the motivation and give up easily
Affective	Feelings of stress and anxiety a child may experience can hinder their success in overcoming challenges
Selection	How children choose the way to tackle the challenge within their capability

> **CASE STUDY 2.3**
>
> When her adoptive parents met with the Head Teacher and Year 1 teacher, Jada's behaviour was discussed. The teacher commented that Jada cannot concentrate, does not want to focus in class and cannot sit still and keep nice hands. When asked how this behaviour was managed, the Head Teacher said that they use their strategy referred to as red cards, and this means that if a child receives a red card, they must stand to the side at break time and watch their peers play. If they receive more than one red card, they must go to nurture group in the afternoon when the creative lessons take place.

Reflective Questions

1. What are your comments/thoughts knowing that Jada has been in the care system?
2. What behavioural strategies would you use if Jada was in your class or school?
3. How do think this language would impact Jada?
4. How would this approach impact Jada and her identity and self-image?
5. Are behavioural policies in schools inclusive?

Stigma

A notable impact on the overall development of CLA is the stigma they face. Stigma, as stated by Goffman (1963), is a term that originated with the ancient Greeks and was depicted as a cut or burn on a person's body to show that that person was different in some way. Goffman (1963) continued to describe how this person's difference can often be enacted in social interactions where people are categorised as being either normal or abnormal and that this difference can then lead to being devalued and socially excluded. Stigma is a social process involving identifying and discriminating against a person or group based on a perception of this difference and Goffman explains that stigma can ultimately result in stereotyping which can lead to discrimination. Roberts (2021) notes that stigmatisation can result in incidents of bullying that can lead to forms of social exclusion, meaning that being in care can be an obstacle for CLA. Research has shown that they experience higher rates of bullying than other children (Dougherty et al. 2013). In other words, stigmatisation generates alienation and is a form of marginalisation.

Many CLA are from groups of our society that may already face marginalisation, for instance, Black, Asian, and other minority ethnic groups, those from different religious backgrounds, children with disabilities, lower socioeconomic groups and those who identify as LGBTQ+ (NICE 2021). As reported by the NSPCC (2024), using data from the Department for Education (DfE 2022) and the Office for National Statistics (2023), in England 6.9 per cent of children looked after are Black, 4.8 per cent Asian, and 72.9 per cent White. It is unclear why some ethnic groups are overrepresented in the care system while others are not. Since there is no firm evidence to support this claim, we can speculate that there could be many different reasons why this is the case, such as cultural perspectives and values and access to services. This issue can be attributed to a variety of factors that have varying degrees of influence (Owen and Statham 2009). Our professional responsibility is to ensure that we are aware that certain groups of CLA are marginalised and to ensure that their needs are being met to minimise further marginalisation.

It has been noted by Roberts (2021) that professionals in children's services acknowledge widespread stigma, and they believe children are more likely to receive attention if they are well-known within their community. This stigma from professionals also meant the increased likelihood of referring care-experienced children to children's services. Day (2017) in her research found that many CLA are labelling themselves or are labelled by professionals as having mental health concerns if they have demonstrated challenging behaviour and subsequently been referred to mental health services. But is it not expected that some CLA will display challenging and sometimes violent behaviours as a result of the trauma they have endured in their lives?

A recent review by Silver, Golding and Roberts (2015) summarises the poor psychosocial outcomes for CLA; academically, socially and psychologically, with increased mental health problems. It is possible for the stigma experienced during childhood to have long-lasting effects that may persist into adulthood. Compared to adults, children encounter stigma differently and this negatively affects their development of a sense of self. As a result, their interactions and educational achievements may then be affected in a negative way. The educational impact of stigma is a concern as children may struggle in school which further exasperates the likelihood of CLA having lower academic achievement. In order to improve the current and future well-being of CLA, we need to identify whether and how stigma is contributing to this.

> ### Reflective Questions
>
> 1. Consider the effects of stigma. How might negative labels impact an individual's sense of self?
> 2. Do you think parents feel that they are stigmatised if their child is in care?

For many of us, the labels that are given to us throughout our childhood tend to remain for a long time, potentially following us into our adult lives. The power of a label should not be underestimated as it can be considered the catalyst for developing imposter syndrome. Imposter syndrome is when we feel that we do not belong or feel out of place in cultural, social and educational aspects of our society. This could be in the workplace or educational settings. It is also when we feel that others have more of a right to belong in a place than we do, and this is also compounded by the fact that we also feel that others think that we do not belong either. In other words, it refers to a combined sense of inadequacy and inauthenticity (Breeze, Addison and Taylor 2022).

> **CASE STUDY 2.4**
>
> Think back to Arla from Case study 2.2 and imagine that at 26 years old she successfully embarks on her journey into higher education and starts her undergraduate degree to work with children with similar backgrounds to her own. During her first week, Arla encounters many different people from a wide range of backgrounds and starts to feel that she does not belong. A little voice only she can hear repeats that she is "factory material" and she soon starts to feel like an imposter and does not deserve to have a place at university.

Language

There is a lot of discussion about the language we use when we refer to children being looked after by the local authority and this section will explore some of the negative language still being used by professionals and governing bodies. The language and abbreviations professionals use in the care sector reinforce negative connotations (Lewis 2019). In his article in *Community Care* entitled, "The Language of Care Unfairly Labels Children and Professionals Are Complicit", Lewis (2019) argues that the professional language of CLA is negatively impacting children in long-term foster families and that:

> Professionals are complicit in a system which labels children's long-term homes as 'placements', the people that are there to make them feel like family members as 'carers', with their lives openly scrutinised in their presence several times a year by a group of professionals – teachers, social workers, and health representatives at a 'LAC' review.

The NSPCC (2023) states that when children hear words like these, it creates a sense of being different and makes them feel stigmatised. How we discuss and speak to children and about children in care is important and language matters. With this being said, the fostering charity, TACT, has a Language that Cares project to highlight that the label "LAC" needs to be replaced. Fieller and Loughlin (2022) share a similar view on how the language used contributes to the stigmatisation of children in care. They acknowledge that "looked-after children are already disadvantaged educationally, financially, and emotionally. They are often on the receiving end of stigma, epistemic injustice, and social isolation" (Fieller and Loughlin (2022). They argue for a more person-centred focus on language, making it less clinical. It is appreciated that our preferred language removes the stigma and the negative connotations and gives the child a sense of grounding, however, it is a concern if we lose the meaning of words that are currently used.

Summary

CLA are arguably one of our society's most vulnerable groups and the language we use to characterise them is important. Labels mean that others treat us according to them and when labels are reinforced, it becomes harder for us to break free of these labels and we will tend to develop a self-image that matches the particular label. Using the acronym LAC is depersonalising children who are looked after and the language we use unfairly damages their right to be viewed and treated like any other child in our society. Labels position CLA as being different from other non-care-experienced children and make them feel stigmatised. It is important to be mindful that stigma varies across cultural, social, and political contexts and children from different backgrounds face distinct challenges, so professionals need to be aware of these differences. Professionals need to challenge the use of this type of language as it is often associated with harmful stereotypes. As professionals, we need to make sure that we challenge the stigma of CLA, including societal biases and misconceptions. We need to erase the misconception that CLA or care-experienced children will have poorer educational and emotional outcomes than their peers, as this could result in these children engaging in a self-fulfilling prophecy. We have a responsibility to create the right conditions that will enable CLA in care to fulfil their full potential.

References

Bandura, A. (1997). *Self-efficacy: The Exercise of Control*. New York: W.H. Freeman.

Bartlett, S. and Burton, D. (2020). *Introduction to Education Studies*. 5th edn. London: SAGE Publications.

Becker, H.S. (1973). *Outsiders: Studies in the Sociology of Deviance*. 3rd edn. New York: Free Press.

Breeze, M., Addison, M., and Taylor, Y. (2022). Situating Imposter Syndrome in Higher Education. In M. Addison, M. Breeze, and Y. Taylor (eds) *The Palgrave Handbook of Imposter Syndrome in Higher Education*. Cham: Palgrave Macmillan. https://doi.org/10.1007/978-3-030-86570-2_1

Brock, T. (2023). *Welcome to Social Theory*. London: SAGE Publications.

Children and Families Act 2014. Available at: https://www.legislation.gov.uk/ukpga/2014/6/contents/enacted

Cocker, C. and Allain, L. (2012). *Social Work with Looked After Children*. London: SAGE Publications. [eBook]. Available at: *ProQuest Ebook Central* https://ebookcentral.proquest.com/lib/ntuuk/detail.action?docID=5164008.

Dansey, D., Shbero, D., and John, M. (2019). Keeping Secrets: How Children in Foster Care Manage Stigma. *Adoption and Fostering*, 43(1), 35-45. https://doi.org/10.1177/0308575918823436

Day, A. (2017). Hearing the Voice of Looked After Children: Challenging Current Assumptions and Knowledge About Pathways into Offending. *Safer Communities*, 16(3), 122-133. DOI: 10.1108/SC-01-2017-0003

DfE (Department for Education). (2020). Outcomes for Children Looked After by Local Authorities in England. Available at: https://explore-education-statistics.service.gov.uk/find-statistics/outcomes-for-children-in-need-including-children-looked-after-by-local-authorities-in-england

DfE (Department for Education). (2022). Children Looked After In England Including Adoption. Available at: https://explore-education-statistics.service.gov.uk/find-statistics/children-looked-after-in-england-including-adoptions/2023

Dougherty, S., Wolff, E., Ariyakulkan, L., and Serdjenian, T. (2013). Bullying and Children in the Child Welfare System. *Sage Journals*, 43(1). Available at: https://dss.sc.gov/media/1206/bullying.pdf

Fieller, D. and Loughlin, M. (2022). Stigma, Epistemic Injustice and Looked After Children. The Need for a New Language. *Journal of Evaluation in Clinical Practice*, 28, 867–874. DOI: 10.1111/jep.13700

Goffman, E. (1963). *Stigma: Notes on the Management of Spoiled Identity*. Harmondsworth: Penguin Books.

Hargreaves, D. (1967). *Social Relations in a Secondary School*. London: Routledge & Kegan Paul.

Horsburgh, J. (2022). *Improving Outcomes for Looked after Children*. [eBook]. Leeds: Emerald Publishing Limited. https://doi-org.ntu.idm.oclc.org/10.1108/978-1-80071-078-820221002

Lewis, M. (2019). The Language of Care Unfairly Labels Children and Professionals Are Complicit. *Community Care*. https://www.communitycare.co.uk/2019/04/29/the-language-of-care-unfairly-labels-children-and-professionals-are-complicit/

Macblain, S., Dunn, J., and Luke, I. (2017). *Contemporary Childhood*. London: SAGE Publishing.

Mannay, D., Evans, R., Staples, E., Hallett, S., Roberts, L., Rees, A. and Andres, D. (2017). The Consequences of Being Labelled 'Looked-After': Exploring the Educational Experience of Looked-After Children and Young People in Wales. *British Educational Research Journal*, 43(4), 683–699. DOI: 10.1002/berj.3283

Merton, R. (1948). The Self-Fulfilling Prophecy. *The Antioch Review*, 74(3). 75th Anniversary (summer 2016), pp. 504–521. DOI: https://doi.org/10.7723/antiochreview.74.3.0504

NICE (National Institute for Health and Care Excellence) (2021). *Looked-After Children and Young People*. NICE guideline. Public Health England. Available at: https://www.nice.org.uk/guidance/ng205/resources/lookedafter-children-and-young-people-pdf-66143716414405

NSPCC (National Society for the Prevention of Cruelty to Children). (2023). Why Language Matters: Why You Should Avoid the Acronym 'LAC' When Talking About Children In Care. Available at: https://learning.nspcc.org.uk/news/why-language-matters/looked-after-children

NSPCC (National Society for the Prevention of Cruelty to Children). (2024). Statistics Briefing Children in Care. Available at: https://learning.nspcc.org.uk/media/4j5nsulc/statistics-briefing-children-in-care.pdf

Office for National Statistics (2023). Ethnic Group by Age and Sex in England and Wales. Newport: Office for National Statistics. Available at: https://www.ons.gov.uk/peoplepopulationandcommunity/culturalidentity/ethnicity/datasets/ethnicgroupbyageandsexinenglandandwales

Owen, C. and Statham, J. (2009). *Disproportionality in Child Welfare*. London: Thomas Coram Research Unit Institute of Education University of London. Available at: https://dera.ioe.ac.uk/id/eprint/11152/1/DCSF-RR124.pdf

Roberts, L. (2021). *The Children of Looked After Children: Outcomes, Experiences and Ensuring Meaningful Support to Young Parents in and Leaving Care*. Bristol: Bristol University Press. DOI: //doi.org/10.2307/j.ctv1jbzchd

Selwyn, J., Wijedasa, D., and Meakings, S. (2014). *Beyond the Adoption Order: Challenges, Interventions and Adoption Disruption*. Bristol: University of Bristol, Department for Education.

Silver, M., Golding, K., and Roberts, C. (2015). Delivering Psychological Services for Children, Young People and Families with Complex Social Care Needs. *The Child & Family Clinical Psychology Review*, 3, 119–129.

Stewart, D. and Harris, T. (2007). Entitlement and Potential: Overcoming Barriers to Achievement. In P. Zwozdiak-Myers (ed.), *Childhood and Youth Studies*. Exeter: Learning Matters.

3
Adverse Childhood Experiences

> **CHAPTER AIMS**
>
> This chapter will explore Adverse Childhood Experiences (ACEs) and present the impact adversity has on Children Looked After (CLA), developmentally, socially, and educationally. By the end of this chapter, you will be able to do the following:
>
> - Explore the origins of ACEs and what these look like today.
> - Understand different definitions of ACEs and what this means for CLA.
> - Reflect on the impact of ACEs on CLA's holistic development, behaviour and attachment.
> - Develop an awareness of ACEs and identify strategies to support children who have been exposed to adversity.
>
> **Keywords**
>
> adverse childhood experiences, awareness, development, impact

Introduction

Adverse Childhood Experiences (ACEs) play an important role in the identity of Children Looked After (CLA). Children who have experienced separation from the family and their home will have experienced one of the recognised ACEs discussed later in this chapter. This chapter clarifies the differences in language when referring to children's ACEs and looks into the historical origins of ACEs with a reflection on how they have evolved to be recognised in today's society. Towards the end of this chapter, we will explore the different responses and behaviours children show as a result of the impact of their adversity.

Definitions of ACEs

ACEs can be simply defined by the name, an event or situation that has impacted a child or children in an adverse manner. However, there are different definitions and interpretations of ACEs, depending on the professional who is applying this term. According to the NHS (2023), ACEs are potentially traumatic and highly stressful events or situations which occur in early childhood or adolescence. This can be associated with a single or prolonged series of events which influence a child's feeling of safety, security, trust and belonging. Scott (2021) develops this further by explaining that ACEs affect children both mentally and physically, which can have a significant influence on children into adulthood.

With this definition in mind, it is often difficult to decipher whether a child has been a victim of ACEs as these can often be subjective to the child who has experienced or is experiencing them. To understand what an ACE is and how it impacts a child's life, it is first important to explore what the different things are that can be considered adverse.

Origins of ACEs

The first ACE study was conducted by Felitti et al. (1998) who investigated the impact of childhood events and situations of trauma on children in the immediate and longer term in life (Figure 3.1). A survey of ten questions was developed with five items discussing child abuse and neglect as well as five items reviewing family background and situations, such as violence, alcohol and substance abuse, loss of family members, illness and incarceration. Each time a participant answered "yes" to the experience identified, a point was given which at the end of the survey gave the person a score from 0 to 10. The survey was used retrospectively to assess the number of ACEs children had experienced between birth to their 18th birthday.

The findings of this study were particularly interesting as they revealed that the higher the ACE score, the higher probability of children experiencing adversity and poorer outcomes in adulthood (Frederick, Spratt and Devaney 2021). As the number of adverse experiences increases, so does the risk for smoking, alcoholism, drug abuse, depression, suicide attempts, multiple sexual partners, sexually transmitted diseases, heart disease, cancer, chronic lung disease, skeletal fractures, and liver disease.

Despite the initial research conducted on ACEs still being relevant to children and adults today, it is only natural that the original ten ACEs have been developed to be relevant to

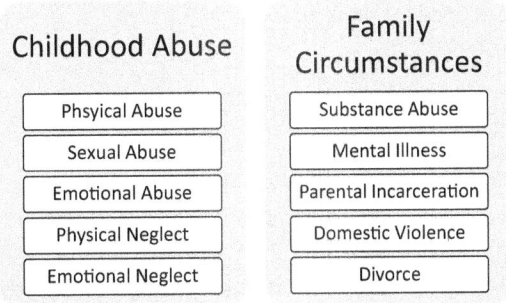

Figure 3.1 The ten original ACEs

Source: Felitti et al. (1998).

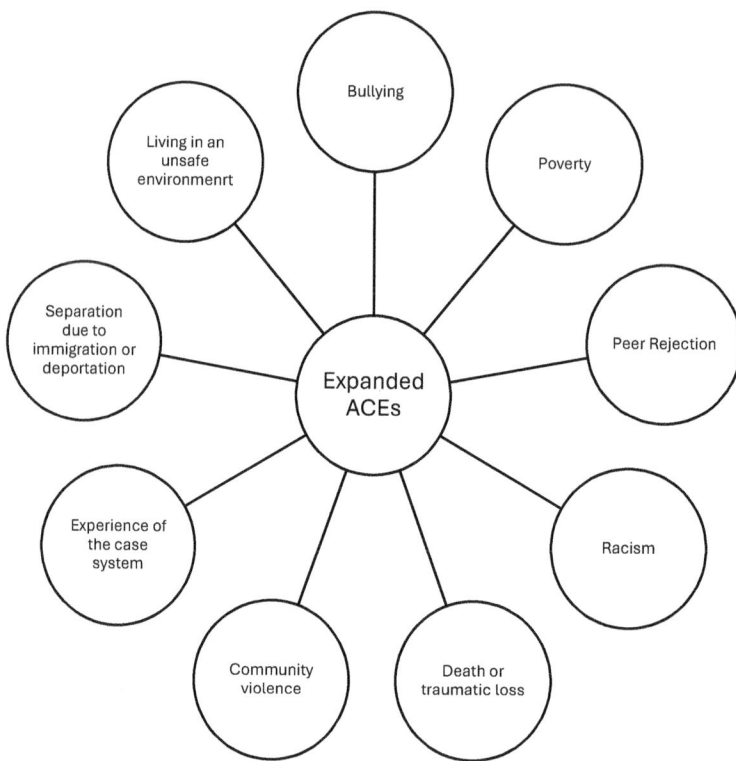

Figure 3.2 Expanded ACEs
Source: Karatekin and Hill (2018).

today's society and contexts. Additional categories have been proposed to reflect the experiences of children living in diverse urban environments that were not reflected in the original ACE questions. Even though these additional ACEs were not accepted as part of the traditional ten ACEs, they are often included as part of the Expanded ACEs screening questions. Figure 3.2 presents the different features which are now accepted as creating an adverse childhood experience for children.

CASE STUDY 3.1

Daniel is a 3-year-old who lives at home with his single mum since they were 2 weeks old. Daniel's mum receives state benefits and has recently been relocated into supported living accommodation following the eviction from their rented housing. Mum has limited access to funds from her state benefits and must provide everything for herself and Daniel and receives no additional support from Daniel's birth father. Daniel has an identified child in need plan and has regular contact with a social worker to improve the living conditions at home.

CASE STUDY 3.2

Sienna is 8 years old and lives with her grandparents following the incarceration of her parents at the age of 6. Her grandparents take care of Sienna with support from the local authority welfare services. Sienna has an official contact arrangement to visit her parents in prison but often cannot go due to the long distance involved.

CASE STUDY 3.3

Haiyat is 14 years old and has lived in the UK for 6 years after fleeing their home country to escape conflict. They came to the UK with mum, dad, and younger sibling. Last year Haiyat's mum passed away due to complications in childbirth. Due to political reasons, dad has been deported, leaving Haiyat and their sibling classed as "unaccompanied children". Both children are in temporary care of the local authority and have been assigned foster families to help bring stability and structure to the children's lives.

Reflective Questions

1. Reflect on one of the above case studies and consider the potential of the child being impacted by an identified ACE.
2. Is the child being exposed to more than ACE?
3. How do you think this identified ACE or ACEs will impact the child in the short term and the long term?
4. What do you think will happen to the child next?

ACE Statistics in the United Kingdom

The most recent studies in the UK identify that almost 50 per cent of adults have experienced one ACE and 14 per cent of adults have experienced four or more ACEs before reaching the age of 18 (Welsh Government, 2021; Public Health Institute, 2020). These statistics raise several concerns, first, that the latest of these statistics is 2021, suggesting that for in Wales and England, no further studies into ACEs have been conducted. The number of children who have experienced ACEs could have significantly increased in this time. Another concern is that the lack of recent statistics could also imply a lack of concern from the governing authorities about the impact ACEs have on children and their life outcomes. The difficulty in gaining statistical knowledge on the adversity that children have experienced is based on the ability to recognise ACEs and report them. When it comes to memories of adversities during childhood, people may not always be able to recall them accurately or may not consider them to be adverse, especially if the event was a common occurrence.

Despite our knowledge of childhood adversities and vulnerabilities, we do not have a clear and accurate understanding of how prevalent they are, for example, there could be more than 50 per cent of people who have experienced an ACE in childhood but have yet to report or recognise the ACE. However, studies have shown that ACEs are more common among people who reported a low socioeconomic status in childhood, with a small number of children having lived in deprived areas in England and Wales (Bellis, Lowy and Leckenby 2014).

ACEs and Children Looked After

CLA are commonly exposed to very high rates of ACEs, as discussed earlier, ACEs are defined as physical, sexual, emotional abuse and neglect, as well as living in unsafe surroundings, being exposed to domestic violence, having parents with mental health issues or drug or alcohol dependency, and experiencing family dysfunction (Webster 2022). CLA may not have been exposed to all the ACEs identified earlier, but the removal of a child from the family home is only done after an investigation and a genuine belief that a foster placement would be better for the child. Removing a child from their family home is likely to expose a child to a further ACE and the trauma that is associated with this. However, it is believed that, with the appropriate support, love and care, children will be able to overcome this traumatic experience. However, Trivedi et al. (2021) claim removing children from their family home can cause unnecessary trauma for them, and that children are better off remaining in their home. Yet despite the large number of children being subjected to abuse and neglect in the family home, the Office of National Statistics (2024) identifies that 27 per cent of the children are looked after by the local authority because there is not a suitable parent or adult to care for the child, in which case the child is better off in the care of the local authority.

In 2023, in England, 83,840 children were recorded as being looked after by the local authority (Office of National Statistics 2024). Some 65 per cent of these children are looked after due to being at risk of abuse or neglect, 13 per cent due to family dysfunction, 9 per cent due to parent abandonment, and 7 per cent because the family were unable to meet the child's basic needs. A further 7 per cent of looked after children had no suitable parent to provide for them, 5 per cent because of the child's or parent's disability or illness and 1 per cent of looked after children is due to anti-social behaviour. These statistics are reflective of the ACEs identified in the original and expanded ACEs discussed earlier, however, they also show that the most common reason for children being looked after by the local authority is due to abuse or neglect.

Impact of ACEs

During early childhood, a child's experiences shape the way their brain develops and lay the foundation for their learning and development (Gilmore, Knickmeyer and Gao 2018). Trotta, Murray and Fisher (2015) state that children who have experienced significant early life adversity face more challenges in their development than those who have not. Positive and negative experiences in a child's early life have a major impact on their brain development. Even though children develop neurologically, hormonally, and immunologically when they are raised in a safe, stable, and nurturing environment, experiencing trauma and chronic stress can adversely affect these development processes (Fond, Haydon and Kendall-Taylor 2015).

Developed by Rutter et al. (1976), Cumulative Risk Theory states that a child's outcomes depend on the number of adverse events a child experiences, such that multiple adverse events result in poorer outcomes than single events. In a similar scoring process to the ACE study, the Cumulative Risk Theory prescribes a number to each event or exposure to a risk factor resulting in harm or trauma to a child. Rutter et al. (1976) proposed that children at significant points in their lives are more likely to deal with a constellation of events or risk factors at one given time rather than isolated risks or adversity. For example, a child who is exposed to neglect is also likely to be exposed to poverty, living in an unsafe environment and maybe even mental health or substance abuse. The results of the theory in practice identify that children who have exposure to multiple risk or adverse events demonstrate more upset and worse outcomes than those who have experienced fewer risks.

Throughout childhood and into adulthood, the stress experienced from ACE exposure can influence how children process information, make decisions, and interact with others. Figure 3.3 shows the transitional impact ACEs have on children between conception to death and this is the order in which these will be explored in the next sections of this chapter.

Disrupted Neurodevelopment

The brain is the central organ involved in perceiving and adapting to adversity and stress. Research on the neurological effects of ACEs on brain development shows that changes in brain growth and development can occur in response to stress. Exposure to childhood adversity may impact children's development and lead to the recalibration of different brain systems because of abuse and neglect, which may make children more vulnerable to mental health issues later in life (Conkbayir 2023). The stress on brain structures can have cumulative "wear and tear" effects, including changes in brain architecture that may or may not be reversible (Conkbayir, 2023). We will examine this in more detail in Chapter 4.

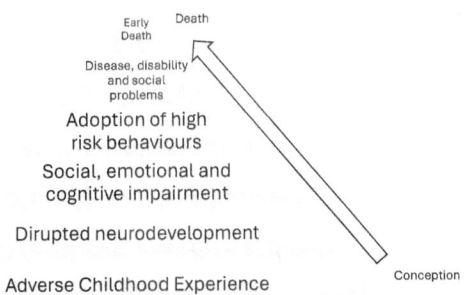

Figure 3.3 The pyramid showing the impact of ACEs

As a result of ACEs, the prefrontal cortex, the hippocampus, the amygdala, and other areas of the brain involved in self-regulation and emotion may be negatively impacted, whereas nurturing experiences, such as positive parenting, encourage normative brain development despite ACEs (Rollins and Crandall 2021). Attention, perception, and working memory (becoming aware of information while using it) are vital components of information processing for children. Children who have been exposed to ACEs have difficulty listening, concentrating, and following instructions, as key brain regions, such as the prefrontal cortex, hippocampus, and limbic system, are compromised by their neurobiological impact (Conkbayir 2023). This inevitably plays a crucial role in how children learn in school and education settings.

Impact on Cognitive Development and Learning

The brain is the central organ involved in perceiving and adapting to adversity and stress. Blodgett and Lanigan (2018) identified that children who had exposure to even one ACE were at risk of poor academic outcomes, with the risk increasing with every additional ACE. A relationship can be seen between school-based concerns, such as behaviour, attendance and academic output, and the number of ACEs identified in children. The more ACEs a child experiences, the higher the percentage of students with academic concerns increases. Evans et al. (2020) state that children who are exposed to ACEs are less likely to attain the expected level of education at age 6–7 years (Key Stage 1) and age 10–11 years (Key Stage 2). According to Hardcastle et al. (2018), children with ACEs more than double the risk of leaving school with no qualifications and are at much greater risk of unemployment.

Education plays a crucial role in determining individuals' long-term socio-economic outcomes, influencing their life course. Early cognitive development can be adversely affected by psychological changes that result from chronic childhood stress from ACE exposure which will impact on a child's ability to learn and concentrate in the classroom. Hardcastle et al. (2018) report that children exposed to three or more ACEs had lower academic and literacy skills and more teacher-reported behaviour concerns.

Emotional and Social Development

A child who has experienced ACEs and trauma will predominantly function from their limbic system, which makes it difficult for them to operate from their more rational "upstairs" brain. This suggests that children in moments of stress or heightened emotion are more likely to respond in more physical ways (Conkbayir 2023). Children who have experienced ACEs may struggle to communicate their needs, feelings, and emotions to those around them. We also need to remember that children may have experienced angry, violent, and aggressive events or relationships and this could influence the way they communicate with others. Some children may respond in loud, angry, vocal communications, others may be silent.

It is also important to keep in mind that children exposed to ACEs may have difficulties in self-regulating. The reasons for this are often a lack of healthy role models for

Adverse Childhood Experiences 35

self-regulating provided by their primary caregivers, along with chronic hyperarousal. This often leaves children struggling to judge the social cues presented to them in different situations but also exposing them to an uncomfortable vulnerability of not being able to read the social situation which inevitably heightens feelings of anxiety and stress (Van Tieghem et al. 2021).

In addition to difficulties forming relationships with peers, children who lack trust in their environment are more susceptible to anxiety and depression. However, despite the fact that the relationship between exposure to ACEs and anti-social behaviour, such as violence, is well established, other familial, social, and economic outcomes have been less well examined, making it difficult for professionals to recognise a child's experiences of ACEs.

High-Risk Behaviours

High risk behaviours are any actions that increase the likelihood of developing a negative or undesirable outcome on a child's health and well-being. Many behaviours are considered high risk, with some of the most common shown in Figure 3.4.

CLA and children who have been maltreated have a significantly higher risk of engaging in these behaviours. In a study of high-risk behaviours and ACEs with children aged between 9 and 11 years old, Garrido, Weiler and Taussig (2018) reported almost 20 per cent of children claimed they had behaved violently, 13 per cent of children had used substances, and slightly more than a third reported delinquency. Almost half of the children had indicated they had engaged in at least one of the common high-risk behaviours identified above. Males were significantly more likely than females to engage in violence and delinquency, but there were no significant sex differences in rates of substance use. Slightly

Figure 3.4 High risk behaviours

more than half of males had engaged in at least one high-risk behaviour, in comparison to a third of females within the study.

All children who had participated in this study were CLA at some point in their lives but what is alarming from this study is the age of the children who participated. When reviewing the common high-risk behaviours identified, these are what are usually associated with adolescent teenagers, however, the children who had participated in the study were significantly younger than this, with large numbers of them having exposed themselves to a high-risk behaviour. This reiterates the need for professional support for CLA who have experienced ACEs in an attempt to minimise children engaging in high-risk behaviours.

Disease, Disability and Social Problems

Even before conception, during in utero development, and into childhood, adversity can negatively impact physical and mental health. The effects of stress and adversity on the nervous system and autoimmune system weaken children's resilience to disease over time as cortisol levels in the brain increase (Conkbayir 2023). Studies show that as the number of ACEs a child has been exposed to increases, the higher is the risk of developing poor health. Some disability and diseases, such as obesity, cancers and heart conditions, can stem directly from the engagement of high-risk behaviours, such as eating disorders, smoking, drug, and alcohol use. Other disabilities, such as poor mental health, including depression, post-traumatic stress disorder, anxiety and social anxiety, can be a direct impact of the exposure of the ACE itself (Austin et al. 2016). Research suggests that around 45 per cent of CLA have a diagnosable mental health disorder, and up to 70–80 per cent have recognisable mental health concerns (York and Jones 2017).

The impact of these types of disabilities and diseases on children and young people can significantly affect their ability to socialise with their peers and in different situations. Physical disabilities can impact a person's ability to engage in the physical world outside of the treatment facilities and their homes, and mental health concerns can prevent the child from effectively socialising with their peers and in social situations. Anderson and Clarke (2022) state that many CLA who have recognised disability, even mildly, are often worried, unhappy and isolated from their peers. Among the children in the research study, mental health concerns are four times higher than among children who are not CLA, the most common feelings impacting children's mental health are worry, depression, fear, lack of self-confidence and self-esteem (Anderson and Clarke 2022).

Reflective Questions

1. *Think back to your case study, how do you think they are doing in nursery or school?*
2. *What challenges might they face in education?*
3. *Do you think they will have made friends and built relationships?*
4. *What is the potential impact on these children?*
5. *How far up the ACEs pyramid do you think these children may be?*

Case Studies Revisited

> **CASE STUDY 3.1 REVISITED**
>
> Despite regular intervention work from the social worker, Daniel's mum has been unable to meet his basic needs at home. Daniel has been placed in foster care with a small family who have one older teenage child. A contact agreement has been set up for Daniel's mum to see him at a contact centre once a week where they can play together. However, she has missed some visits and was late to some. This left Daniel feeling very confused and upset.

> **CASE STUDY 3.2 REVISITED**
>
> Sienna's grandparents are regularly being called into school as Sienna struggles to concentrate in class and other children are distracted by this in class. Sienna is desperate to see her mum but the distance is too much for her grandparents to take her. Because of this, Sienna has started to get angry and aggressive at not being able to go. Social workers have become more active with Sienna but Sienna is reluctant to share her feelings and emotions with them.

> **CASE STUDY 3.3 REVISITED**
>
> Haiyat and their sibling have been reallocated to new foster families. The previous foster family were no longer able to care for both children. Due to the shortage in foster families in the local area Haiyat and their sibling have been separated and are now living with different families. They see each other every two weeks at the park for about an hour and Facetime twice a week.

Reflective Questions

1. Can you identify any further ACEs that the children in the case studies have now experienced?
2. Where on the ACEs pyramid would you place each of the children?
3. Why have you attributed this section of the pyramid to this child?
4. What strategies would you apply to help support these children to decrease the likelihood of the child moving further up the pyramid?

ACE Awareness

As previously discussed, CLA will have been exposed to one or many ACEs and traumatic situations or events. A child who has experienced early trauma and has not formed strong attachments to the adults around them is likely to feel uncomfortable and mistrustful when adults are trying to establish a key person relationship with them. It is maintained that what children with ACEs require is the room and space to grow and heal from trauma, with time to develop relationships and form attachments and trustful relationships with those responsible adults when they are ready. CLA are likely to instinctively resist relationships, as because of their trauma, children have missed out on the building blocks of care and attachment, resulting in lack of trust in caregivers and inability to attune with others. It is therefore important to develop strategies to support them in both social and educational settings and situations.

It is important that children are accepted for what they are and feel valued despite their current situation or background. For CLA, simple expectations of routine, having to wait, being asked to share or play nicely, are likely to lead to them feeling unwanted, unliked or the adult providing the instruction thinking that they are a bad child. Without intentionally doing so, the professional is building a further emotion of distrust between themselves and the child.

Children who have experienced a difficult start in life may learn that the world is not a safe place, and people in it cannot be trusted to keep them safe. It is impossible for children to learn and explore if they do not feel safe and secure. CLA often do not believe they deserve care and attention and may feel deep shame. These feelings and assumptions about the world underpin all the interactions they have with professionals and their peers.

The work of Stephen Porges (2016) helps us to understand what happens when a child feels that they are in danger or in an unsafe environment. His polyvagal theory suggests a hierarchy of three levels (Figure 3.5).

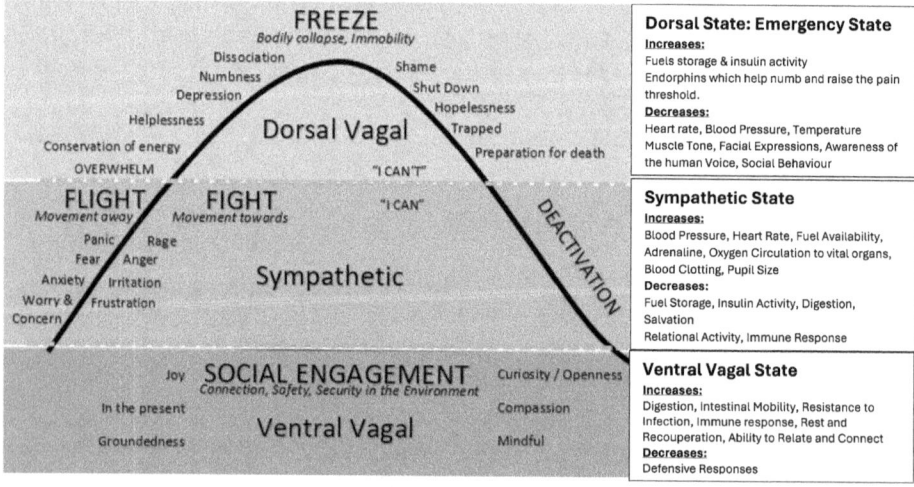

Figure 3.5 Porges' (2016) polyvagal theory

When children do not feel safe, the body prepares itself to react to the danger. If the danger is high, the nervous system reacts in a way that mimics a *freeze* state. Porges describes this as a time of great stress for a child, and they may appear to zone out and present confusing or inappropriate behaviour, such as laughing uncontrollably, sleeping or disassociation. To professionals who do not understand CLA's background, the situation may not appear dangerous, but for a child who has experienced ACEs, certain situations may trigger a freeze response. Something seemingly harmless like the noise of a bin lorry driving past or a police officer walking past the setting gates could trigger a danger warning and a freeze response from a child who associates loud noises or police officers with dangers or threats.

When children identify a threat, but it is not at the highest level, their bodies prepare themselves for defence, which we call *flight or fight*. Children who have experienced ACEs may escalate to this state very quickly without warning or any noticeable trigger to cause this. It could be that an everyday event or a certain situation may trigger a response as the child, due to their ACE, associates the trigger with potential danger or harm, for example a doorbell ringing could trigger the child to perceive potential danger at the door. The reaction to fight is to prepare themselves to confront the danger, leading to displays of anger and rage, whereas the reaction to flight may mean that the child may hide, run away and panic at the situation.

ACE Strategies

PACE

The PACE approach (**P**layfulness, **A**cceptance, **C**uriosity and **E**mpathy) is a key strategy for supporting CLA, it was developed by American psychologist Dan Hughes. The PACE approach can help children regulate their emotions and reflect on the meaning of these frustrations, helping the professional to communicate with the child about their feelings. The key word of acceptance allows the child to feel a sense of unconditional love which is the foundation of building positive attachments and support strategies for CLA. The key principle is to connect with the child and redirect the situation through PACE. When a child is upset, the professionals connect with them emotionally, then once the child is more in control and receptive, they can be redirected to something away from the situation that triggered them.

Hughes (2018) breaks PACE down into the following areas:

- *Playfulness* is to enjoy being together, being light-hearted and displaying interest, curiosity and fun with the child. Playfulness reduces the shame that a child may feel from something going wrong but also focuses the child away from bad things happening to a positive relationship with the professional applying PACE.
- *Acceptance* is vital to the safety of CLA, as it allows the relationship to be developed between professional and child without judgement. It secures a safe space for children to express their feelings and to understand the reasons behind their feelings and emotions.

- *Curiosity* is important, as it allows children to be curious about their feelings, thoughts and wishes. CLA find trusting others difficult, and through curiosity this opens them up to explore whether they are able to trust the professional with whom they are sharing their feelings and experiences. Professionals use curiosity to create a space where children are able to ask questions but also where the professional can ask questions to explore the behaviour and emotions of the child, for example, "I wonder why this happened…?"
- *Empathy* shows that the professionals are able to understand children's feelings and emotion. Professionals are showing they are trying to understand the CLA they are supporting and offering them reassurance will show the child that they care and are invested in the positive well-being of the child.

Loving Pedagogy and Professional Love

Page (2018) developed the concept of professional love to understand the type of care and affection professionals display to children in their settings. As previously discussed, it is important for CLA to have positive reactions to their individual situations, behaviour and emotions. These reactions must be able to effectively meet their need for safety and security which is often through nurturing and intimate responses. The concept of professional love suggests that professionals should feel comfortable to enact loving practices such as hugging and sensitive touch to build secure positive attachments with children. Where there is lack of secure relationship with the caregiver for CLA, this approach helps the child to develop a loving, secure, attached relationship with a different appropriate adult (Szeintuch 2020).

The concept of professional love has also been developed by Grimmer (2021) who explores loving pedagogy in early childhood practice. Grimmer explains that building secure attachments with professionals takes time for all children, but more so for CLA as they have not always experienced a loving and nurturing home environment. When a child finds it difficult to form attachments and show love, it is important for professionals to show how they feel through positive interactions, behaviour and engagement. This places importance on the impact these actions have on developing CLA attachments, as CLA may not have had consistency of affection and warmth, and have experienced a lack of reaction to their needs being met by the adults closest to them. The consistent application of loving pedagogy over time allows CLA to develop trust in the responses and actions of professionals and can help to form positive attachments with carers who follow similar approaches. Grimmer (2021) reiterates that when professionals understand how children like to be loved, they will better understand the child, leading to building and maintaining a strong attachment with them, which results in children learning more effectively.

Summary

This chapter has provided an in-depth exploration of ACEs and the role they play in the lives of CLA. We have reviewed ACEs both historically and contemporarily not only to explore the development of ACEs over time but also to understand the impact they have on children's holistic development. The most important takeaway from this chapter is the understanding of different strategies that we can apply to our own professional practice in supporting CLA and some key ways we can help children navigate through their life journey.

References

Anderson, E. and Clarke, L. (2022). *Disability in Adolescence*. London: Routledge.

Austin, A., Herrick, H., Proescholdbell, S., and Simmons, J. (2016). Disability and Exposure to High Levels of Adverse Childhood Experiences: Effect on Health and Risk Behavior. *North Carolina Medical Journal*, 77(1), 30-36.

Bellis, M.A., Lowey, H., and Leckenby, N. (2014). Adverse Childhood Experiences: Retrospective Study to Determine Their Impact on Adult Health Behaviours and Health Outcomes in a UK Population. *Journal of Public Health*, 36, 81-91. DOI: 10.1093/pubmed/fdt038

Blodgett, C. and Lanigan, J. D. (2018). The Association Between Adverse Childhood Experience (ACE) and School Success in Elementary School Children. *School Psychology Quarterly : The Official Journal of the Division of School Psychology, American Psychological Association*, 33(1), 137-146. https://doi.org/10.1037/spq0000256

Conkbayir, M. (2023). *Nurturing Children's Resilience Following Adverse Childhood Experiences: An Adult Guide*. London: Routledge.

Evans, A., Hardcastle, K., Bandyopadhyay, A., Farewell, D., John, A., Lyons, R.A., Long, S., Bellis, M.A., and Paranjothy, S. (2020). Adverse Childhood Experiences During Childhood and Academic Attainment at Age 7 and 11 Years: An Electronic Birth Cohort Study. *Journal of Public Health*, 189, 37-47.

Felitti, V.J., Anda, R.F., Nordenberg, D., Williamson, D.F., Spitz, A.M., Edwards, V., Koss, M.P., and Marks, J.S. (1998). Relationship of Childhood Abuse and Household Dysfunction to Many of the Leading Causes of Death In Adults. The Adverse Childhood Experiences (ACE) Study. *American Journal of Preventative Medicine*, 14(4), 245-258. DOI: 10.1016/s0749-3797(98)00017-8. PMID: 9635069

Fond, M., Haydon, A., and Kendell-Taylor, N. (2015). Communicating Connections: Framing the Relationship Between Social Drivers, Early Adversity and Child Neglect. Available at: http://frameworksinstitute.org/early-childhooddevelopment-and-adversity.html

Frederick, J., Spratt, T., and Devaney, J. (2021). Adverse Childhood Experiences and Social Work: Relationship-Based Practice Responses. *The British Journal of Social Work*, 51(8), 3018-3034. DOI: https://doi.org/10.1093/bjsw/bcaa155

Garrido, E.F., Weiler, L.M., and Taussig, H.N. (2018). Adverse Childhood Experiences and Health-Risk Behaviors in Vulnerable Early Adolescents. *Journal of Early Adolescence*, 38(5), 661-680. DOI: 10.1177/0272431616687671. Epub 2017 Jan 12. PMID: 29861530; PMCID: PMC5976451

Gilmore, J.H., Knickmeyer, R.C., and Gao, W. (2018). Imaging Structural and Functional Brain Development in Early Childhood. *Nature Reviews Neuroscience*, 19(3), 123.

Grimmer, T. (2021). *Developing a Loving Pedagogy in the Early Years*. Abingdon: Routledge.

Hardcastle, K., Bellis, M.A., Ford, K., Hughes, K., Garner, J., and Ramos Rodriguez, G. (2018). Measuring the Relationships Between Adverse Childhood Experiences and Educational and Employment Success in England and Wales: Findings from a Retrospective Study. *Public Journal of Health*, 165, 106-116. DOI: 10.1016/j.puhe.2018.09.014

Hughes, D. (2018). *Building the Bonds of Attachment: Awakening Love in Deeply Traumatized Children*. 3rd edn. London: Rowman & Littlefield.

Karatekin, C. and Hill, M. (2018). Expanding the Original Definition of Adverse Childhood Experiences (ACEs). *Journal of Child and Adolescent Trauma*, 12(3), 289-306. DOI: 10.1007/s40653-018-0237-5

NHS. (2023). Adverse Childhood Experiences (ACEs) and Attachment. Available at: https://mft.nhs.uk/rmch/services/camhs/young-people/adverse-childhood-experiences-aces-and-attachment/

Office of National Statistics. (2024). Children Looked After in England Including Adoptions. Available at: https://explore-education-statistics.service.gov.uk/find-statistics/children-looked-after-in-england-including-adoptions

Page, J. (2018). Characterising the Principles of Professional Love in Early Childhood Care and Education, *International Journal of Early Years Education*, 26(2), 125-141. DOI: 10.1080/09669760.2018.1459508

Porges, S. (2016). Trauma and the Polyvagal Theory: A Commentary. *International Journal of Multidisciplinary Trauma Studies*, 1, 24-30. DOI:10.3280/IJM2016-001003

Public Health Institute. (2020). Evaluation of a System-Wide Approach to Implementing Routine Enquiry about Adversity in Childhood. Available at: https://www.ljmu.ac.uk/-/media/phi-reports/pdf/07-2020-nottinghamshire-reach-evaluation--interim-report-june-2020.pdf

Rollins, E.M. and Crandall, A. (2021). Self-Regulation and Shame as Mediators Between Childhood Experiences and Young Adult Health. *Frontiers in Psychiatry*, 12, 1-9.

Rutter, M., Tizard, J., Yule, W., Graham, P., and Whitmore, K. (1976). Isle of Wight Studies, 1964-1974. *Psychological Medicine*, 6(2), 313-332.

Scott, K. (2021). Adverse Childhood Experiences. *InnovAiT*. 14(1), 6-11. DOI:10.1177/1755738020964498

Szeintuch, S. (2020). Social Love: The Power of Love in Social Work. *Australian Social Work*, 75(4), 471-482. DOI: 10.1080/0312407X.2020.1742755

Trivedi, G., Pillai, N., and Trivedi, R. (2021). Adverse Childhood Experiences and Mental Health: The Urgent Need for Public Health Intervention in India. *Journal of Preventive Medicine and Hygiene*, 62, E728-E735. DOI:10.15167/2421-4248/jpmh2021.62.3.1785

Trotta, A., Murray, R., and Fisher, H. (2015). The Impact of Childhood Adversity on the Persistence of Psychotic Symptoms: A Systematic Review and Meta-Analysis. *Psychological Medicine*, 45, 1-18. DOI:10.1017/S0033291715000574

Van Tieghem, M., Korom, M., Flannery, J., Choy, T., Caldera, C., Humphreys, K.L., Gabard-Durnam, L., Goff, B., Gee, D.G., Telzer, E.H., Shapiro, M., Louie, J.Y., Fareri, D.S., Bolger, N., and Tottenham, N. (2021). Longitudinal Changes in Amygdala, Hippocampus and Cortisol Development Following Early Caregiving Adversity. *Development Cognitive Neuroscience*, 48, 1-11.

Webster, E.M. (2022). The Impact of Adverse Childhood Experiences on Health and Development in Young Children. *Global Pediatric Health*. 9. DOI:10.1177/2333794X221078708

Welsh Government. (2021). Review of Adverse Childhood Experiences (ACE) Policy: Report. Available at: https://gov.wales/review-adverse-childhood-experiences-ace-policy-report-html

York, W. and Jones, J. (2017). Addressing the Mental Health Needs of Looked After Children in Foster Care: The Experiences of Foster Carers. *Journal of Psychiatric and Mental Health Nursing*, 24(2), 143-153.

4

Trauma and Neurodiversity

CHAPTER AIMS

In this chapter, we will examine what the neurodiversity paradigm has to offer individual Children Looked After (CLA) and their families. By the end of this chapter, you will be able to do the following:

- Understand the concept of neurodiversity and how it is reshaping societal views.
- Explore traditional theories of disabilities and the development of the brain.
- Understand the challenges faced by neurodivergent CLA.
- Celebrate the diversity and strengths that neurodivergent children have.

Keywords

neurodivergent, neurodiversity, neurotypical, serve and return, social and medical models of disability, strength-based approach, toxic stress

Introduction

The concept of neurodiversity has reshaped the way in which society perceives children and young people who think, learn and behave differently. Definitions of common terms concerning neurodiversity and what it means to be neurodivergent will be discussed, as well as an overview of the many types of neurological differences that constitute neurodiversity. In light of this, traditional theories of disability, as well as social, medical and social constructivism, will be the basis of your own professional reflection. When discussing the development of the brain, we need to appreciate how neuroscience has helped the early childhood and the children's sector as a whole in an understanding of how early experiences can shape or ultimately break the neural connections in the brain development of babies and young children. Evidence from developments in neuroscience and advances in the technology used to see how the brain works have proved what many, if not all, early childhood pioneers have been theorising for decades, if not centuries. Further challenges that many CLA with a neurodevelopmental disorder face are being misdiagnosed or over-diagnosed as well as facing problems in accessing appropriate support and interventions. Ultimately, what we would like you to take from this chapter is the notion that our differences need to be celebrated and treated as strengths rather than deficits.

The Concept of Neurodiversity

There has been an increased interest in neurodiversity as a concept in the past few years, despite the fact that the concept itself is not new. It is thought that the term was coined during the 1990s by autism activists in an attempt to shift the focus from the medical view of autism and the notion that a cure could be found through treatment to a more holistic approach to the illness. In those days, the term "disability" was mainly used to describe people with physical, mental, or intellectual impairments. Since then, there has been a great deal of progress in our understanding of how neurological disorders, such as autism, ADHD, and bipolar disorder are perceived by the general public. Botha et al. (2024) suggest that the shift in our use of technology, including the emergence of the World Wide Web, has acted as a vehicle to raise awareness of the many differences we have as humans. Due to this raised awareness, we have begun to see the possibility of categorising ourselves in different ways, not only according to our ethnicity, gender, class, or disability but also according to the ways in which we learn, think and behave differently. It has been through the internet that people with all kinds of disabilities have been able to form communities and share their experiences of being misunderstood and mistreated, as well as their narratives about their experiences. The internet has certainly brought together people who are often socially isolated from each other, and it has given them all the ability to speak for themselves. In recent years, this momentum has grown at a rapid rate, and it has started to embed itself in the social justice agenda through legislation and policies relating to disability and equality. In the past few years, neurodiversity has quickly become a well-known concept that is being incorporated into policies and procedures, not only in the educational sector but also in the wider children's sector as a whole.

We have seen a significant shift in the language we use when referring to people with what was previously referred to as learning disabilities or hidden disabilities. In the first place, the word disability does not work well as a general term, for the simple reason that it is overly general in nature. It is also a word that is associated with stigma, where the word is often associated with a distinct feeling of "I'm normal and you're not."

Before we continue, we need to understand a few terms relevant to this topic. Table 4.1 presents some definitions.

There are many types of neurological differences that constitute neurodiversity. These include attention deficit hyperactivity disorder (ADHD), autism, dyslexia, dyspraxia,

Table 4.1 Definitions of neurological terms

Terms	Definition
Neurodivergent	Having a brain that differs significantly from the average
Neurodiversity	The diversity of our brains and minds
Neurotypical	Having a brain that develops and functions in a societal typical way

dyscalculia and specific language impairments, to name but a few. In the United Kingdom, ADHD is considered one of the most common neurodevelopmental disorders in childhood (NHS 2024). Our brains are all unique in the way they function, and each one is unique in its own way. Each of us receives and processes information differently, so our behaviour will differ based on the manner in which we process and receive information. In a nutshell, neurodiversity is concerned with how we think, how we learn and how we behave. The differences in thinking, learning, and acting are not deficiencies or deviations; they are just examples of the fact that there are different ways to think, learn, and behave. It is estimated that approximately 1 out of 7 people in the United Kingdom have some kind of neurological difference (NHS 2024). Figure 4.1 presents some examples of the types of neurological differences you may come across in your professional roles with children.

The shift to using neurodiversity as an umbrella term for these wide-ranging neurological differences is helping to strengthen the neurodiversity paradigm. Society is now starting to realise and understand that neurodiversity is naturally occurring and operates like other equality and diversity dimensions. When using the term "neurodiverse", it needs to be noted, however, that the use of the word "diverse" in this sense does not equate to unusual or rare and therefore should not be used when referring to an individual. A group can be neurodiverse, but an individual cannot. As previously discussed in Chapter 2, using the correct terminology matters and the correct use of language will help avoid stigmatisation around special needs. We also need to reflect on the labels we may use when discussing children who fall into neurological groups and who at some point in their lives are going to

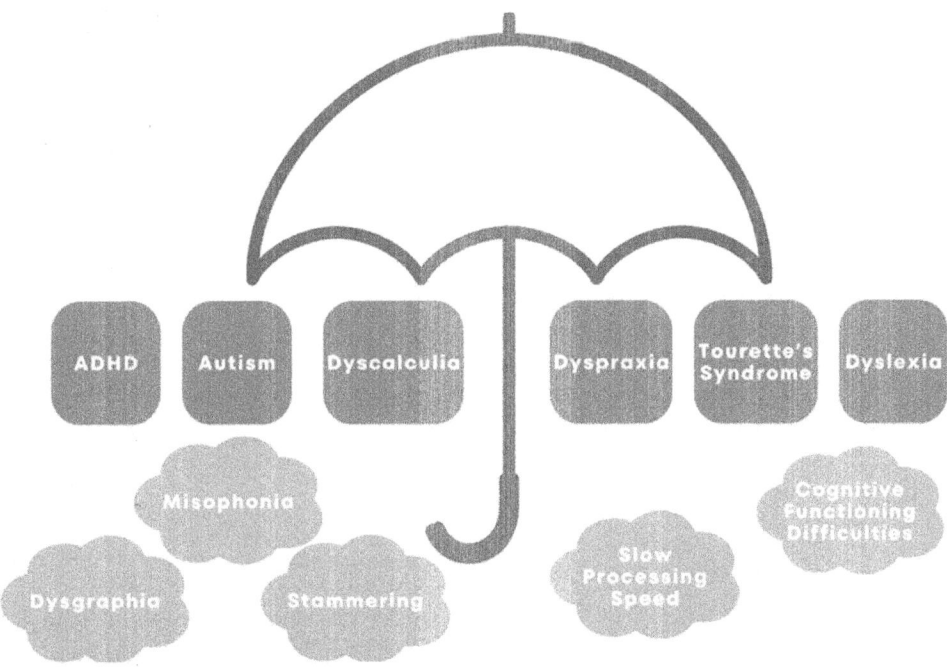

Figure 4.1 Examples of types of neurological differences

be classified as neurodivergent and are going to have a label attached to aid understanding and enable them to receive the appropriate support that they need.

> **Reflective Questions**
>
> 1. What does neurodiversity mean to you?
> 2. How do you embrace neurodiversity with the children you work alongside?

> **Reflection**
>
> The following excerpt is based on an experienced educator's personal reflection.
>
> As a trainee further education teacher nearly two decades ago, I had many students who were both diagnosed and undiagnosed, with a few of the most common Special Educational Needs or learning difficulties. I adapted my teaching resources to help support their learning. These were often autism and dyslexia. However, many of the terms used have now been replaced by the more specific terms listed under the neurodiversity umbrella. The number of terms has increased, which as well has made me, as an educator, more aware of the many different ways we all think, learn and behave. Additionally, I also believe that this has helped me to understand and appreciate all the differences we have as individuals. The expansion of the neurodiversity paradigm has helped shift educational professionals' views and encouraged neurodiversity to be recognised in a more positive light. Personally, I think this movement is having and will continue to have a lasting impact on what we view as being different.

> **Reflective Questions**
>
> 1. What are your thoughts about this?
> 2. Is this a positive step towards inclusion in our society?
> 3. Do you believe the movement towards embracing neurodiversity will have a lasting impact on society's perception of differences?

Models of Disability

It can be useful to be aware of and understand the underpinning concepts of different models of disability to help illustrate why there is often a continued societal perception and attitudes towards children and young people with developmental differences. The *social model of disability* conceptualises disability not as a problem related to a person's physical, intellectual, or mental condition, but as a consequence of the way our society is structured. People who are disabled are inherently disabled by society. The social model of disability focuses on the following aspects: societal barriers, equality and inclusion, empowerment and agency, shift in social perspectives, social justice, and shift in the social paradigm of disability. The social model of disability emphasises that disability is created by social and environmental factors, and society can alleviate the disadvantages experienced by people with disabilities by removing or changing these factors (Menendez and Gelman 2024).

In contrast, the *medical model of disability* views disability as a problem that must be treated, cured, or managed through medical intervention. As a result of this medical model, there is a stigma associated with people with disabilities who need to have their condition fixed. In contrast, the social constructivist view of disability suggests that people's disabilities are constructed through their social interactions, cultural norms and societal structures. As a result, social, historical, and cultural contexts influence our understanding of disability and advocate for the recognition and value of diversity in society.

The Anna Freud National Centre for Children and Families, in their guide to neurodiversity in the early years (2023), offers information about another model called the *neurodiversity-informed model*. This model considers the need for increased emphasis on a child's particular interests, differences and needs as well as offering support that is child-led. The main focus of this model is to view the child as an expert and recognise that their voice is valued with the embedded notion that we should not deny what the difficulties or needs are but rather have a better understanding of what they are.

> *Reflective Questions*
>
> 1. Which model do you agree with more and why?
> 2. In what ways does the social model of disability empower individuals with disabilities compared to the medical model?
> 3. How does the social constructivist view of disability explain the role of cultural norms in shaping our understanding of disability?
> 4. How can changing social perspectives on disability lead to broader social justice outcomes?
> 5. How can these models be applied to CLA to recognise and support their unique needs and strengths?

Neurodivergence can be genetic, the result of early trauma, or a combination of the two. Studies of the brain have shown that people with neurodevelopment disorders are "wired" differently. ADHD, for example, is a complex disorder and is accounted for by both genetic and environmental factors with the most common factor being premature birth, low birth rate and maternal substance abuse during pregnancy (Faraone et al. 2015). With this in mind, our understanding of the functions of the brain and how early trauma can have long-lasting consequences on the future of the child needs to be addressed.

Toxic Stress

Early experiences in childhood have a direct impact on the development of the brain architecture which provides the building blocks for all future learning, behaviour, and health. If these experiences are adverse, as discussed in Chapter 3, these negative effects can be carried into adulthood. It is estimated that there will be more than one million neural connections formed every second during the first 1,001 days of early childhood, which is the period from conception to the child's second birthday, with the development of the brain's architecture starting even before birth and continuing throughout adulthood (Center on the Developing Child at Harvard University 2024). As a result of the experiences that children are exposed to, they can build connections that in turn help maintain a healthy brain function.

In discussions about the concept of building brains, the phrase *serve and return* is often featured and it refers to the responsive interactions between children and the adults in their lives who take care of them and respond appropriately to their needs. This turn-taking interaction is where a child will instigate an interaction which we can call a serve. This can be in the form of a sound or an expression, for instance, and the adult then responds to that particular serve and returns it in a positive way to the child. As a result of this back-and-forth interaction, we show we have actively listened to our children through their actions and then responded to them in a way that was positive and supportive. With these serve and return interactions with children, we will be able to lay the foundation for all future learning and help all children develop the skills they need to deal with the challenges they may face in life, as well as build the foundations for future learning. There is no doubt that the serve and return dynamic plays an important role in supporting healthy emotional, social and mental development.

> **CASE STUDY 4.1**
>
> Sofia is in her pushchair, and she notices a man walking a dog coming towards her. Immediately, she leans forward and reaches for the dog with both hands, babbling softly as she reaches for it. There is a sense of excitement in her facial expression when she sees this dog for the first time. The father of Sofia does not notice this serve and continues to push Sofia past the dog without taking note of it.
>
> This one missed opportunity for Sofia's father to return the serve in this case will not result in detrimental and long-lasting effects on her future learning and health. However, if attention is not paid to what children are focused on repeatedly throughout their early childhood, it can adversely affect their learning and health.

Reflective Questions

1. Do you think that professionals working in the children's sector are aware of these serve and return interactions and how crucial they are to supporting brain development?

> 2. How can parents balance their responsibilities while still being attentive to their child's interests?
> 3. What advice would you give to a new parent about the importance of being responsive to their child's interests?

It is important to note that in the absence of a responsive parent or carer, the brain's architecture does not form as it should, which then has a detrimental effect on the child's learning, behaviour, and health in general. In spite of this, the future architecture of the brain cannot be determined by the mere presence of a responsive parent or caregiver alone. In addition, children need a mixture of cognitive, social, and emotional support to further strengthen the brain's building blocks to avoid unsteady foundations that can eventually cause the building blocks to collapse in the future. It is important to remember that stress is an important component of healthy development for children, and being able to cope with stress can have a large impact on the way their body responds with the fight or flight response. It is impossible for us to control a child's environment or their experiences in a way that minimises their potential for stress, but we can support them in managing this stress in the best way possible. The development of neural connections can be affected if children are unable to deal with the stress in their lives and remain in a high state of stress for prolonged periods of time, thereby resulting in toxic stress. This often has lifelong consequences. A positive and supportive relationship between adults and children as well as a safe, nurturing and supportive environment can be conducive to the child's well-being during times of extreme stress. This means that the child's stress response will be conducive to their healthy development if the adults are able to calm the child during those times.

According to the Center on the Developing Child at Harvard University (2024), there are different responses to stress as identified in Figure 4.2.

As a result of more negative experiences in childhood, the more toxic stress response we experience in childhood, the greater the likelihood that we will experience developmental delays and health conditions such as diabetes, heart disease, substance abuse, and depression in the future. This supports the myriad of child development theorists who have previously contested that early childhood is the most important time in a child's life. In the absence of good support in place to act as a scaffold to prevent the building blocks in a child's brain from collapsing, the child's future will be seriously affected as they grow into adulthood.

Children Looked After

As discussed in Chapter 3, Adverse Childhood Experiences (ACEs) are traumatic experiences that CLA are more than likely exposed to. For instance, parental exposure to poor nutrition, postnatal abuse, family stress and violence, to name a few, all of which are well documented as negatively affecting children's development, including emotional, cognitive, and behavioural aspects. The early years of a child's life are critical for brain development and early exposure to traumatic experiences will affect them in later life (DfE 2019).

50 Advocating for Children Looked After

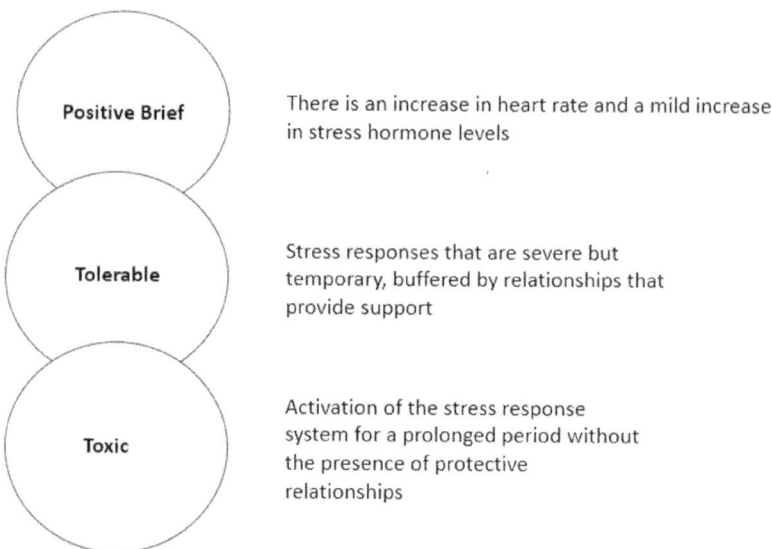

Figure 4.2 Overview of different responses to stress

In CLA, mental, behavioural and developmental disorders are highly prevalent (McAuley and Davis 2009). Yet, according to Ogundele (2020), there is limited research into the neurodevelopmental profile of CLA. Only half of the children who had needed to be supported by a social worker between 2012 and 2017 were able to achieve a good level of development within their early years compared to the three-quarters who had no welfare services support. In agreement with this, Willis, Dhakras and Cortese (2017) claim that ADHD has been researched extensively in the wider population but not in CLA.

The field of neuroscience has evolved, and we now have a better understanding of the biological functions of conditions, such as autism, ADHD and other neurodevelopment disorders. The prevalence of some of these neurological disorders is increasing globally, possibly due to improved diagnostic testing and awareness. However, there is startling research that suggests that this prevalence has increased within the CLA population (Parsons et al. 2019). In their research, Heady et al. (2022) asked experienced social workers about their perceptions and opinions concerning neurodevelopment disorders within the CLA population. A key finding is misdiagnosis and over-diagnosis whereby one participant commented that a child who entered foster care with an ADHD diagnosis soon started to settle down and was reassessed by their doctor. This diagnosis was removed along with the label, however, it is more concerning that this child had been prescribed medication from a very early age when in fact there was no need. Another participant claimed that it is easier to label and medicate CLA rather than take the time to consider the actual cause of their behaviour and, in the children's sector, there is a concern about the over-diagnosis of ADHD symptoms. However, other neurodevelopment disorders are often overlooked, such as autism, dyslexia, and dyspraxia. Hull and Mandy (2017) state that this is because many CLA with fewer behavioural problems are frequently not diagnosed. Conversely, Heady et al. (2022) offer the reason that, for medical professionals, it is difficult to separate the very often complex needs of children who have experienced ACEs, which include social, emotional, and behavioural symptoms, from the symptoms of ADHD which may lead to confusion and the inability to diagnose children correctly. While some neurodevelopmental disorders can be diagnosed with a medical test, others such as ADHD can only be diagnosed based on the behaviour shown.

As previously discussed in Chapter 2, labelling and categorising a child are controversial, however, CLA will more than likely have an array of labels already and an added diagnostic label can sometimes be of benefit. For instance, if a child has been given a diagnostic label this could support their well-being, especially if carers and educators are aware and adapt their support according to the needs of the child. This could improve the child's educational attainment and achievement. However, it needs to be stated that this diagnostic labelling of a child could have the opposite effect completely. For instance, this label may hide potential underlying difficulties or trauma for which the child may need support.

Another challenge faced by neurodiverse CLA includes not having appropriate access to service provision. We have already discussed the importance of early identification and interventions in improving outcomes for children with neurodevelopmental disorders and that a diagnosis means that that child will now have direct access to the specialist support that is needed, yet this is not always the case (Legg and Tickle 2019). Access to diagnostic assessments, mental health services and other forms of support such as educational psychologists, are difficult to obtain for any child and their family and for CLA the often-frequent changes in residential care, foster families and schools further compound this.

Arguably, we should not be making assumptions that CLA who have experienced trauma are neurodiverse. In this sense, we should be making sure that all CLA or care-experienced children have a neurodevelopmental assessment. It is also important to note that assumptions such as these can lead to a CLA not being diagnosed with common neurodevelopment disorders such as autism and not receiving the appropriate support needed (Pinto 2019). However, emerging research within the field of neurodevelopment disorders has shown higher prevalence rates for children looked after compared with their peers (Willis, Dhakras and Cortese, 2017).

Reflection

According to the Department for Education (DfE 2019), children who have needed a social worker at some point in their lives do significantly worse than their school peers at every stage of their educational journey. Those children who needed social care services were reported as being 50 per cent less likely to achieve a strong pass in their English and maths GCSEs.

> Reflective Questions
>
> 1. What about those children who are neurodivergent?
> 2. What do their educational outcomes look like?

Strategies for Neurodiverse Children

As professionals, it is important to understand children's diverse abilities as it helps promote not only a nurturing and positive environment in which children feel safe and secure but also helps us to identify any learning barriers that require early interventions. We can also support children by providing personalised learning experiences which will help children to be successful. There are several strategies that can be implemented to support all children, including those that are CLA:

- creating neurodiverse spaces
- forming relationships with CLA
- positive reinforcement
- knowing a child's triggers.

Knowing a CLA's triggers is especially useful in identifying potential patterns in a child's behaviour and understanding what has caused these changes. When we know what triggers a child's dysregulation, we can make huge strides in trying to minimise these.

Positive Aspects of Neurodiversity

Neurodiversity enriches our society with so many different positive aspects and by embracing neurodiversity, we can promote a culture of diversity that empowers everyone. Neurodivergent children have the unique strength of being able to think from a unique perspective which means they can present us with fresh ideas that often challenge the traditional way of doing things. Figure 4.3 presents a few positive attributes that neurodiverse children and young people may possess.

Focusing on the strengths, skills and talents that neurodivergent children have will improve the lives of the children we work alongside as it encourages a more understanding environment in which children can thrive and reach their full potential. Leaf Complex Care is a healthcare provider that aims to change how our society perceives neurodiverse children and adults and part of their provision is implementing this strengths-based approach to aid the creation of a culture that focuses on "what's strong" rather than "what's wrong" (Leaf Complex Care 2024). This ideology is crucial in changing the view that society has on these children and young people. When working with neurodivergent children, the prompts in Figure 4.4 help us to focus on their strengths, skills and interests.

Autism

- Focus and passion for unique interests, creative and artistic talents, strong memory skills, mathematical abilities

Tourette's Syndrome

- Enhanced cognitive control, acute perception, increased energy, empathy and humour

Dyslexia and Dyscalculia

- strong reasoning, puzzle-solving and oral comprehension abilities, increased imagination and creativity, exceptional communication skills, emotional intelligence and empathy

ADHD

- hyperfocus, increased energy, increased problem-solving skills, creativity.

Figure 4.3 Positive attributes of neurodivergent children and young people

Interests	What do they like to play with? Do they show repetitive behaviours or actions? Do they have a special interest? Do they have special comforters?
Strengths	What are they good at? What do they like to play with? What physical skills do they use? What do they choose to do?

Figure 4.4 Prompts to aid focus on strengths, skills and interests

---

Reflective Questions

1. What other prompts can, or do you use?
2. How will knowing this information help you to support further the children you may work alongside?
3. How will this make a difference to the child and wider society?

Organisations for Schools, Young People and Families

Table 4.2 shows a few of the organisations that provide a range of services to help and support families across the United Kingdom, so that children get the best start in life.

Table 4.2 Organisations and services to support CLA

Organisation	Website	Description of services
Barnardo's	www.barnardos.org.uk	Supports children and young people in need of help, advice or a loving home
Salvesen Mindroom Research Centre	www.salvesen-research.ed.ac.uk	Combines current research and practice that benefit children and young people with learning difficulties and their families
The Mix	www.themix.org.uk	A charity that provides free, confidential support for young people under 25 via online, social and mobile
Young Minds	www.youngminds.org.uk	A charity that supports children and young people's mental health
ADDISS	www.addiss.co.uk	National Attention Deficit Disorder Information and Support Service
The ADHD Foundation	www.adhdfoundation.org.uk	Charity offering a strengths-based service for a range of neurological disorders
National Autistic Society	www.autism.org.uk	A charity that supports autistic people and campaigns for improved rights
British Dyslexia Association	www.bdadyslexia.org.uk	Aims to influence government and other institutions to promote a dyslexia-friendly society that enables dyslexic people of all ages to reach their full potential
Movement Matters	www.movementmattersuk.org	An organisation committed to making research accessible to individuals with dyspraxia and their families
I CAN	www.ican.org.uk	A children's communication charity supporting the development of speech and language

Summary

Neurodiversity refers to the variations in the human brain relating to learning, attention, mood and other functions, suggesting that no two minds are the same. Understanding the nuances of neurodiversity helps us as professionals to understand not only ourselves but others more profoundly. As professionals, understanding neurodiversity helps us appreciate the richness of human experiences and fosters a more inclusive and respectful approach to mental and physical health. We need to have dedicated preventative early childhood services as we know that early childhood constitutes a critical period in brain development and exposure to traumatic experiences will have profound effects on CLA's cognitive, social, and emotional development. We are not claiming that all neurodevelopmental disorders are due to environmental factors, however, we need to be vigilant in our understanding of how children's brains form and develop. As this chapter has discussed, CLA are more vulnerable and the need for early support to prevent what we know will happen is crucial. CLA who also have a neurodevelopmental disorder face many challenges, therefore, appropriate identification and diagnosis of these conditions must be carried out. This positive view of neurodiversity shows how our society is advancing in our perception of the neurodivergent child, not only in altering what we perceived as deficits before we now perceive as strengths that mark the uniqueness of individuals. We need to celebrate neurological differences, boost self-esteem, recognise mental health issues and offer support for all children, including CLA who are one of the more vulnerable population in our society.

References

Anna Freud National Centre for Children and Families. (2023). *A Guide to Neurodiversity in the Early Years: Best Ways to Support Children who Have Developmental Differences*. Available at: https://www.annafreud.org/resources/under-fives-wellbeing/a-guide-to-neurodiversity-in-the-early-years/

Botha, M., Chapman, R., Giwa Onaiwu, M., Kapp, S. K., Stannard Ashley, A., and Walker, N. (2024). The Neurodiversity Concept Was Developed Collectively: An Overdue Correction on the Origins of Neurodiversity Theory. *Autism*, 28(6), 1591-1594. https://doi-org.ntu.idm.oclc.org/10.1177/13623613241237871

Center on the Developing Child at Harvard University. (2024). Brain Architecture. Available at: https://developingchild.harvard.edu/science/key-concepts/brain-architecture/

DfE (Department for Education). (2019). Children in Need of Help and Protection: Data and Analysis. Available at: https://www.gov.uk/government/publications/children-in-need-of-help-and-protection-data-and-analysis

Faraone, S., Asherson, P., Banaschewski, T., Biederman, J., Buitelaar, J.K., and Ramos-Quiroga. J. (2015). *Attention-Deficit/Hyperactivity Disorder*. Cham: Springer Nature Limited. Available at: https://www-nature-com.ntu.idm.oclc.org/articles/nrdp201520#citeas

Heady, N., Watkins, A., John, A., and Hutchings, H. (2022). The Challenges that Social Care Services Face in Relation to Looked After Children with Neurodevelopmental Disorders. A Unique Insight from a Social Worker Perspective. *Adoption & Fostering*, 46(2), 184-204. https://doi-org.ntu.idm.oclc.org/10.1177/03085759221100585

Hull, L. and Mandy, W. (2017). Protective Effect or Missed Diagnosis? Females with Autism Spectrum Disorder. *Future Neurology*, 12(3), 159-169.

Leaf Complex Care. (2024). Neurodiversity in Children: Embracing and Supporting Individual Differences. Available at: https://leafcare.co.uk/

Legg, H. and Tickle, A. (2019). UK Parents' Experiences of Their Child Receiving a Diagnosis of Autism Spectrum Disorder: A Systematic Review of the Qualitative Evidence. *Autism*, 23(8), 1897-1910.

McAuley, C. and Davis, T. (2009). Emotional Well-Being and Mental Health of Looked After Children in England. *Child and Family Social Work*, 14(2), 147-155.

Menendez, D. and Gelman, S. (2024). Children's Biological Causal Models of Disability. *Cognitive Development*, 70. Available at: https://www-sciencedirect-com.ntu.idm.oclc.org/science/article/pii/S0885201424000339?via%3Dihub

NHS (National Health Service). (2024). Attention Deficit Hyperactivity Disorder. Available at: https://www.nhs.uk/conditions/attention-deficit-hyperactivity-disorder-adhd/

Ogundele, M. (2020). Profile of Neurodevelopmental and Behavioural Problems and Associated Psychosocial Factors Among a Cohort of Newly Looked After Children In an English Local Authority. *Adoption and Fostering*, 44(3), 255-271.

Parsons, S., McCullen, A., Emery, T., and Kovshoff, H. (2019). Awareness within Local Authorities in England of Autism Spectrum Diagnoses of Looked After Children. *British Educational Research Journal*, 45(1), 364-367.

Pinto, C. (2019). Looked After and Adopted Children: Applying the Latest Science to Complex Biopsychosocial Formulations. *Adoption and Fostering*, 4(3), 294-309. DOI: 10.1177/030857591856173

Willis, R., Dhakras, S., and Cortese, S. (2017). Attention-Deficit/Hyperactivity Disorder in Looked-After Children: A Systematic Review of the Literature. *Current Developmental Disorders Reports*, 4(3), 78-84.

5

Attachments and Relationships

> **CHAPTER AIMS**
>
> This chapter will explore the importance of positive attachments and relationships for Children Looked After (CLA) and the impact this can have on children's future development and outcomes. By the end of this chapter, you will be able to do the following:
>
> - Understand the origins of attachment theory and how this has developed over time.
> - Identify different attachment styles.
> - Explore the impact of attachment and secure relationships for CLA.
> - Identify some key strategies to promote positive attachment for CLA in practice.
>
> **Keywords**
>
> adverse childhood experiences, attachment, children looked after, relationships

Introduction: What is attachment?

Attachment plays an essential role in the healthy growth and development of children from conception. Prenatal attachment can determine the quality of the attachment the child will have when they are born (Golmakani et al. 2020). How children form and maintain attachments has been researched and developed since the early 1900s and is still as prominent today as it was then. To review attachment and what this looks like for CLA, we first need to understand attachment in all its definitions. Different professionals have different definitions of attachment for children and it is therefore important to take care when you are referring to attachment in specific contexts.

In order to properly introduce this chapter, we will provide an overview of different definitions and perspectives of attachment. The Department for Education defines attachments as being a child's innate drive to seek proximity to a protective adult for survival (DfE 2014). This suggests that attachment, in their educational opinion, serves no further purpose than to keep children safe and is the actions of the child and not the adult that ensure

DOI: 10.4324/9781032716978-5

positive attachment. According to the NSPCC (2023), attachment is a "clinical term" which is used to portray the way humans connect to each other through bonds and relationships. The use of the word "clinical" implies a medical or health approach to attachment and this is supported by the *British Journal of General Practice* that states that attachment is an emotional relationship that unites families and because of these relationships, attachment prepares children for independence into adulthood (Rees 2007). This definition contradicts that of the Department for Education (DfE 2014) as this places ownership of building positive relationships back on the families of children. According to Smith, Cameron and Reimer (2017), writing in the *British Journal of Social Work*, attachment refers to the creation of meaningful relationships that extend beyond family life to professional relationships and significant people in a child's life. This suggests that attachment is relevant to all caregiving relationships in a child's life, including relationships between extended family, foster and adoptive parents and other professionals. Thus, there is varying complexity between the different definitions, and of those provided, the definition of attachment outlined in the *British Journal of Social Work* is best aligned with our work with CLA.

Why Is Attachment Important? Origins of Attachment Theory

The origins of attachment theory date back to the 1960s–1970s through the work of John Bowlby. Bowlby proposed that there is an innate drive for children to form emotional attachments with their primary caregivers in their first year of life (Partridge, Maguire and Newman-Taylor 2022). The strength and quality of these attachments would depend on the quality of parenting, the parents' ability to respond to the needs of their child and being able to interpret children's signals. Bowlby stated that children will learn to self-regulate and control their emotions by following the lead of their mother, and, in doing this, the mother creates a safe space for the child, to allow the child to learn independence from the mother and support healthy development and relationships with others in the future (Raby and Dozier 2019).

Bowlby's (1979) overall key findings of attachment theory state that children have shown a clear preference for closeness to their primary caregiver and this relationship is critical to human development (Boldt, Goffin and Kochanska 2020). Babies and young children have an innate drive to source safety and security from their primary caregivers (Sroufe 2016) and as children develop into adulthood, the need for this closeness slowly decreases (Neaum 2022). Children's ability to form strong attachments with adults relies on the adult's ability to respond to infants' feeling of anxiety or distress, as well as the demonstration of affection and love towards the child (Sroufe 2021). Attachment is therefore affected when children do not experience healthy nurturing relationships in early childhood, then children will struggle to form positive relationships not only with parents but also with others such as practitioners, teachers, their peers and friends (Boldt, Goffin and Kochanska 2020).

Children use their attachment with their caregiver as a reference point for deciding what is safe and unsafe (Hirst 2005). Children learn to interpret and understand the expressions and reactions of their caregiver and in turn react accordingly to situations and learn to make judgements for themselves in relation to their safety and security. Attachment is seen as a two-way process, by having a responsive and positive relationship with their caregivers, children learn to trust that they are loved, and deserving of care and protection as well as feeling secure in their environment and surroundings. If the caregiver is unable to meet the child's needs and promote this attached relationship with the child, for whatever reason, then the child feels unsafe.

Ainsworth developed Bowlby's attachment theory further and classified attachment style into one of four categories: (1) secure attachment; (2) anxious attachment; (3) avoidant attachment; and (4) disorganised attachment (McBlain 2022). In each attachment style, the child will demonstrate specific behaviour indicators when around the adults caring for them. Despite there being clear information on the four explicit attachment styles, this does not mean that a child will definitively present as one specific style. Children are unique, and therefore may demonstrate multiple attachment styles at different times (Wurster and Biringen 2023). Next we will discuss the stages of attachment in more detail.

Secure Attachment

Children who experience secure attachment are often children who have experienced love, encouragement, and comfort from the adults around them and therefore the child has built a memory of feeling safe and secure (O'Connor 2017). Secure attachment is mostly observed in healthy families where children form natural connections with their parents as their basic physiological needs are being responded to sensitively and fully (Hughes 2018). For example, when a child is hungry, a parent responds by feeding the child, when a child is upset or hurt, they are comforted by the parent. It is also understood that children can develop secure attachments when they feel safe in their environment and with the adults around them (NSPCC 2023).

However, this suggests that secure attachment does not end when a child has had their nutritional and safety needs met, they also need to have a sense of belonging and a feeling of love through secure and bonded relationships. This can be likened to Maslow's Hierarchy of Needs, implying that for children to develop into independence and adulthood, these basic physiological, safety, love and belonging are required. This was explored in more depth in Chapter 1.

Children who demonstrate a secure attachment style will often find it easier to form relationships with other adults and caregivers, such as professionals, as they have experienced secure and healthy attachments in their home and community. They will feel happy and safe to explore the environment around them as well as showing signs of independence and self-motivation as they have gained confidence in their abilities from the caregivers (Lyu 2023). Children who have developed and maintained secure attachments from infancy to early childhood are shown to have a healthy social and emotional development, an ability to adjust well in new or changing situations and have higher achievement in learning and educational outcomes (Association for Child and Adolescent Mental Health 2020). Figure 5.1 presents some signs which can be used to identify children with secure attachment.

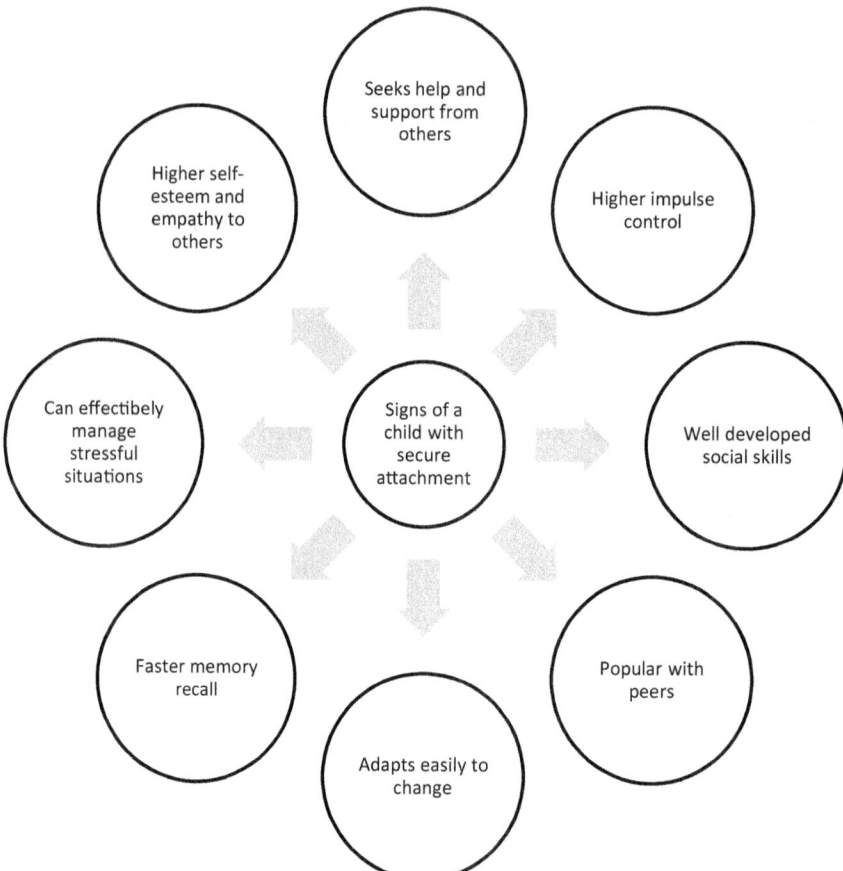

Figure 5.1 Signs of a child with secure attachment

Anxious Attachment

Children who demonstrate signs of anxious attachment have often experienced caregivers being neglectful and dismissive of their unique needs (Rees 2007). Sometimes the parent may be attuned to the child's needs, however, they may be inconsistent in meeting them or responding to the child and providing the safety, security and nurture the child needs to thrive. This leads the child to be confused about their relationship with their caregivers as they have received mixed signals in response to their needs.

A child who is anxiously attached will often display and rely on dramatic emotional behaviour to gain attention from their caregiver in an attempt to get their needs met. This is the child's way of behaving visibly so that the caregiver knows that they should respond to the child. Due to the inconsistent responses from their caregivers, the child can often struggle to understand and build connections with adults, as they are confused by their reactions. This leads the child to behave in a way that will result in the adults providing them

Attachments and Relationships 61

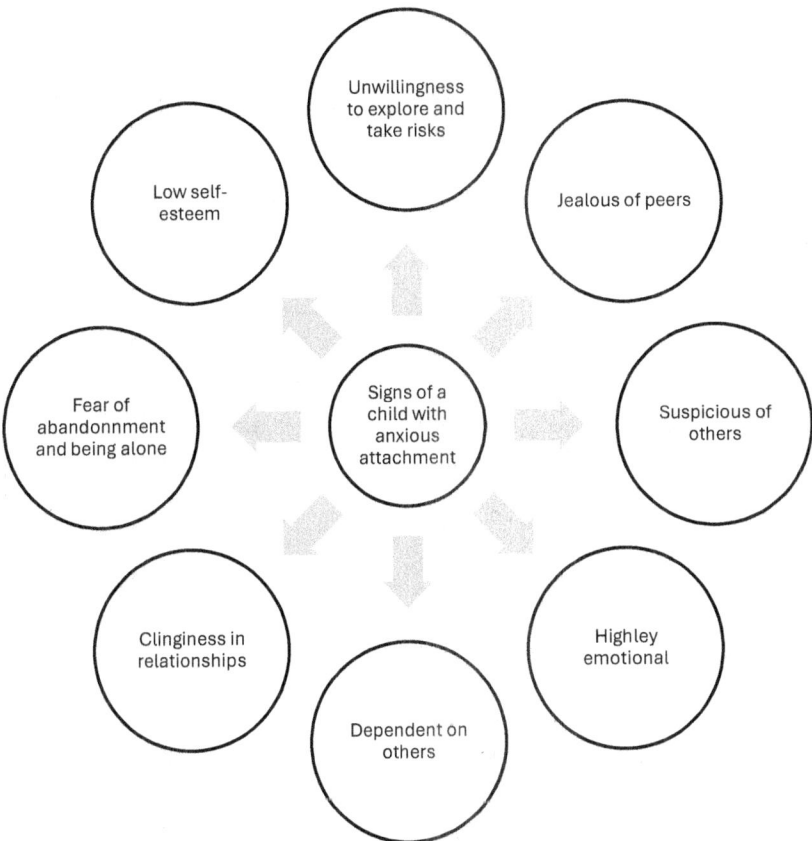

Figure 5.2 Signs of a child with anxious attachment

with positive attention and rewards (Beckes et al. 2021). Figure 5.2 presents some signs to identify children with anxious attachment.

Avoidant Attachment

Avoidant attachment is characterised by the child demonstrating behaviour that lacks emotions and showing little or no reaction when a caregiver leaves and a lack of interest when the caregiver arrives (Wardecker et al. 2020). This can be seen when caregivers are especially strict or demonstrate a lack of emotion with their children. Caregivers expect the child to be self-sufficient and independent, which can lead to a lack of reliance on the caregivers for emotional support and building of relationships. Children demonstrating avoidant attachment may show an inability to regulate their emotions and emotionally respond to situations in the expected way (Lyu 2023), as well as actively seeking to avoid attachment-related situations, such as asking for help or seeking close proximity to adults (Pallini et al. 2019). In contrast to this, children displaying this attachment style may be

62 *Advocating for Children Looked After*

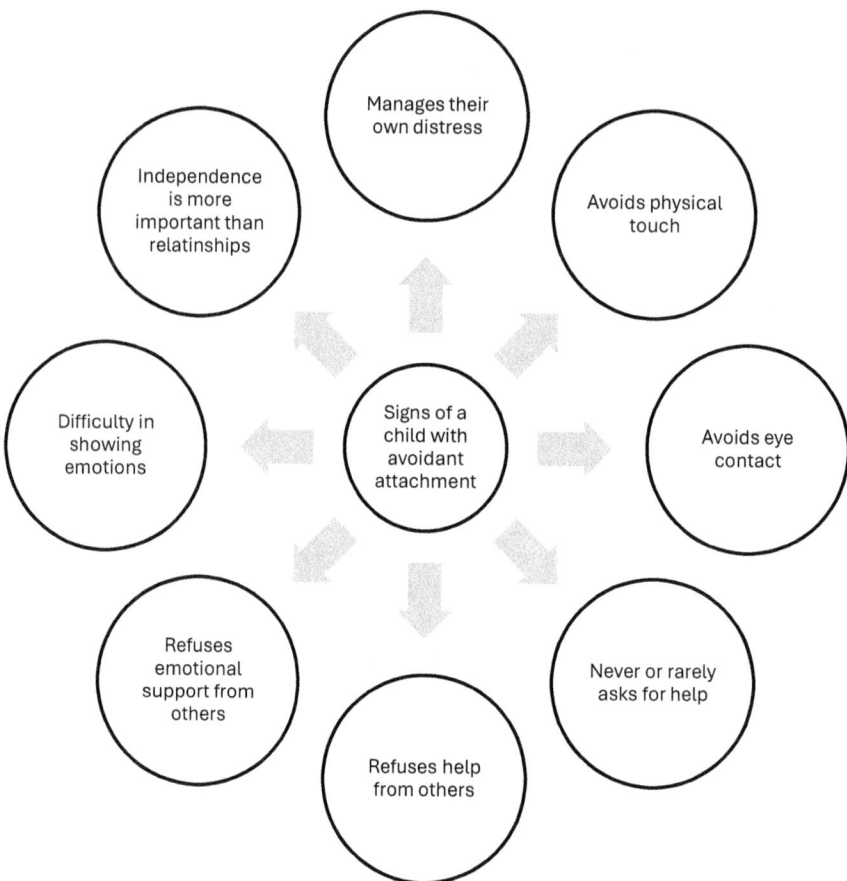

Figure 5.3 Signs of a child with avoidant attachment

overly invested in their environment and their own social world without any attempt to coax responses from adults close by, instead of seeking comfort from the primary caregivers (Strand, Vossen and Savage 2019). Figure 5.3 presents some signs to identify children with anxious attachment.

Disorganised Attachment

Children who show disorganised attachment tend to be those who have experienced the most adverse of backgrounds in their early childhood. It is often expected that children who have been removed from the family home or experienced trauma are highly likely to show disorganised attachment with those around them. Disorganised attachment often means that children struggle to form meaningful attachments, suggesting that they do not have a safe and secure space or person they can relate to (Mackin et al. 2022). Children demonstrating disorganised attachment can be seen to lack confidence and trust in the adults and caregivers around them. They may lack the ability to focus their attention on an activity or concentrate on a specific task for a period of time as their attention may be centred on the environment and the space they are in (Pallini et al. 2019). Disorganised attachment is difficult to identify as children can display conflicting behaviour, for example, the child may become clingy and reliant on adults in the room, or they may avoid the comfort given by adults altogether (Du Paul et al. 2018).

Children who have had prolonged exposure to disorganised attachment are likely to have increased long-term risks of poor mental health due to the distress of their circumstances. Disorganised attachment style increases children's memories of threatening stimuli as well as affecting the children's abilities to cognitively respond to threatening situations. In contrast, children who have had to rely on themselves rather than the positive support of adults are more likely to become fiercely independent adults, suggesting that they will be able to better protect themselves from threatening situations as they can recall these from their childhood. Later in life, outcomes for children who have experienced disorganised, anxious or avoidant attachment styles are often combined with disassociation, Post Traumatic Stress Disorder (PTSD), emotional disconnection, aggression towards peers and low academic achievement (Association for Child and Adolescent Mental Health 2020). It is important as professionals that we can understand and recognise when a child is displaying anxious, avoidant or disorganised attachment styles and put strategies in place to ensure that they receive the best support and ability to build positive relationships to minimise the impact on their learning and development. The case studies give an idea of what a child with each attachment style may do.

CASE STUDY 5.1

Secure attachment: Bailey is 3 years old and attending nursery for the first time. He has completed two settle-in days with his parents. When he arrives at nursery, he is slightly hesitant to leave his mum but as soon as he sees children playing with the trains, he is happy to go and play. When playing outside, Bailey trips and falls, he seeks out the first adult he can find and allows them to comfort him and help care for the bump on his knee.

CASE STUDY 5.2

Anxious attachment: Katie is 4 years old, she is moving from the smaller pre-school room in her setting to the larger one as she is older now than the children she was with. On entering the new room, Katie clings to her key person, and does not want to leave her side. Despite knowing the setting and the others in the room, Katie follows her key person all day, she is encouraged to go and play with the children, but she refuses.

> **CASE STUDY 5.3**
>
> *Avoidant attachment*: James is 5 years old and has been in reception at school for 6 months. When his dad drops him off at school, he walks independently into the classroom. He struggles to take off his coat and bag and becomes tangled. The teacher sees this and offers to help and James says "No" and continues to try and do it for himself. The teacher steps closer to him to help anyway and James backs away from the teacher, insisting he will do it himself despite getting frustrated and not being able to disentangle himself from the bag and coat.

> **CASE STUDY 5.4**
>
> *Disorganised attachment*: Natalie is 6 years old and in year 1 at school. Each morning the children must leave their parents or carers at a certain point on the playground and walk themselves into the class. Each morning Natalie refuses to leave her carer, she becomes distressed and upset. The teaching assistant for her class comes to collect her and walk her in. When in class she takes a little while to settle but she will sit at the edge of the carpet away from her peers as the teacher starts the first activity. When asked a question by the teacher, Natalie is often distracted and not paying attention which can get her into trouble with the teacher. When this happens, she cries and becomes upset but does not allow anyone to comfort her.

Reflective Questions

1. On first reading these case studies would you have recognised and associated each child's behaviour with their attachment style?
2. Do the children show evidence of more than one attachment style?
3. How easy is it to identify the child's specific attachment style?
4. As a professional in the setting, how would you support the child in each of these case studies?

Modern Attachment Theory: Internal Working Model

Since Bowlby's and Ainsworth's introduction of attachment theory, understanding of attachment has developed beyond a child's primary caregiver responding to their basic needs to thrive, as children develop an understanding of themselves and others around them (Howe 2017). As children grow, they develop memories, experiences and feelings about what happens to them when they are with certain people and are placed in different situations, particularly with those they have an attachment to and when they are in need (Skinner and Wellborn 2019). These experiences and memories reflect a child's internal working model, leading them to be able to predict how people they have formed an attachment to around will behave in certain situations (Murphy, Goodall and Woodrow 2020). With this in mind, a child is able to organise how they attach to different people, allowing them to prepare themselves for the response to their actions but also make changes to how they react to people and prevent them from experiencing negativity or anxiety as a result of the relationship and attachments they have built with the people in their lives (Kobak and Bosmans 2019). This means that the child will learn to modify their behaviour in response to the caregiver's behaviour (Gillath and Karantzas 2019).

Reactive Attachment Disorder

A reactive attachment disorder (RAD) is a level of insecure attachment where a child shows a persistent and extensive pattern of behaviour, where they are extremely withdrawn and struggle to form any attachment to their primary caregivers. This can be closely linked to disorganised and avoidant attachment styles and suggests that a child may have experienced severe neglect or lack of response from their primary caregivers (Ellis, Yilanli and Saadabadi 2023). Even in the early stages of understanding attachment, Bowlby and Ainsworth maintained that a child's attachment style is not static, therefore it can change, dependent on their situation and which emotions are triggered by the environment they are in or the people they are with (Bosmans et al. 2020). When placed in situations or with people that they are uncomfortable with, children may exhibit "flight, fight or freeze" behaviours. In these situations, a child may instinctively react to the perceived threat or the things that scare them by retreating to a safe familiar place, confronting, and demonstrating violent behaviour or freezing and not responding to the situation around them (Katz et al. 2021). This is explored in more detail in Chapter 3. These behaviours are often found in children who have experienced trauma and adversity and, therefore, this attachment style plays an important role in how the child forms attachments with those close to them (Hughes 2018). Case study 5.5 explores reactive attachment disorder.

> **CASE STUDY 5.5**
>
> *Reactive attachment disorder*: Liam is a child known to his school as being in and out of local authority care due to the inconsistent care provided by his birth parents. Professionals are aware that there has been at least one time when Liam has been taken from his parents by the police. When in school Liam struggles to concentrate on what's happening in the lessons. He is distracted by loud noises and constantly looking for perceived dangers. When the school bell rings at break and lunch times, Liam shows signs of being extremely scared and frozen on the spot. The teacher reminds him that it is the bell for the break and what that means. Slowly Liam will go outside to join his class but will often stand alone and not join in as if in anticipation of another loud noise.

> *Reflective Questions*
>
> 1. Is Liam's behaviour different to what we would expect from the children in case studies 5.1-5.4?
> 2. As a professional in his setting, what strategies and support would you apply in this situation to help Liam?
> 3. What would you do differently if the child was to respond with flight or fight responses?

Attachment and Children Looked After

Children rely on the adults around them to meet their needs but also to care for them, which is entwined with their development, attachment and ability to succeed as they grow into adulthood (Holmes 2014). The care of children needs to involve elements of love, affection and attachment which many CLA have not received in their childhood. Due to their trauma and ACEs, CLA are likely to have difficulties with trust, and building meaningful relationships as well as a lack of openness for feeling cared for and loved (Cahill, Holt and Kirwan 2016). Becoming a CLA is involuntary and therefore the child may have feelings of oppression by adults claiming to keep them safe, as well as painful past experiences of being let down and trust being violated by those adults (Collins 2018). CLA are therefore more likely to demonstrate insecure attachment styles, whether it be anxious, avoidant, disorganised or reactive, showing signs of this in the case studies.

CLA come from a variety of backgrounds and have a diverse range of experiences of care and love from their family home. No two children will have had the exact same experiences, even if they have been living in the same home and same family as each other (NICE 2021). Children have their own different, specific and individual needs which can be exaggerated because of being a CLA (NSPCC 2023). What is common among all CLA is that they are likely to struggle to form interpersonal, meaningful relationships which can be directly related to the loss and breaks in attachment experienced (Cocker and Allain 2019). Case study 5.6 provides examples of how children from the same family can display different attachment styles.

CASE STUDY 5.6

Sarah, Matthew and Chloe have been in care for 6 months following a long period of social work intervention with their birth family. All three children are living with the same foster family and all go the same school.

Chloe is the youngest child. When going to school she refuses to leave her foster carer and Sarah has to peel her out of the foster carer's arms. Chloe is always upset and can only be consoled by her sister, brother or foster carer. During class, teachers sometimes fetch Sarah from her lesson to assist the teachers in consoling Chloe because she has become upset about something small like moving tables or changing chairs. At break time Chloe actively seeks out her brother as they share the same break time.

Matthew is calm and quiet; the teachers rarely know that Matthew is in the classroom. He does his work quietly and never asks for help he just gets on with whatever he is doing. When Matthew is not able to complete a task or an activity, he becomes frustrated and angry with himself but insists that he does not need help. When the teachers offer to help him, he avoids looking at them and shies away from them.

Sarah is expressive in her class. She is fiercely independent and does not like to be told what to do. She has one or two close friends in her class but does not associate with the others, stating they are "boring and don't understand me". Because of this, Sarah often gets into altercations and arguments with her peers over small things and tells the teachers that she "doesn't want to be friends with them anyway". Sarah is close to her siblings and is always checking up on them but refuses to allow adults close to her to care for her. One time Sarah fell off her chair and teachers could see that she was hurt but Sarah refused to allow the teachers to help and insisted she was "fine".

Reflective Questions

1. *Which attachment styles are shown by which child?*
2. *Why do you think each of the children has developed the attachment style that they have?*
3. *As a professional how would you help to change the disorganised attachment of the children?*

Relationships for Children Looked After

We can see that, as a result of their early experiences, CLA are likely to struggle with relationships with others, however, in order to succeed in their lives, it is important that children are able to alter their attachment style and be able to form meaningful relationships with others. Positive, safe, and stable attachments and relationships help children to develop their self-confidence, self-esteem, and self-reliance and contribute to building a strong sense of identity and belonging, as explored in several chapters in this book. Strong relationships and attachments provide children with a secure person to turn to in a crisis and times of change, as well as provide them with encouragement, positivity, and guidance to support them throughout their life journeys. Long-standing, secure attachments for CLA help children to make sense of their experiences, explore gaps in their own life stories and teach them how to move forward from their ACEs. These securely attached relations are crucial for CLA to develop their identities and be able to build relationships with others in the future.

Strategies for Developing Secure Attachments

Children thrive best when they are in the care of adults who take a genuine interest in them and when the adults allow the child to build those strong attachments to them (Page 2018). With positive attachment being a vital component of children's well-being, it is important that attachment is embedded in children's policy as well as practice (Page et al. 2013).

For children in the early years, the Statutory Framework for the Early Years Foundation Stage (DfE 2023) states each child must be assigned a key person. This is a designated practitioner with whom the child has built a settled relationship and, in turn, the key person is responsible for ensuring the provision is tailored to the child's individual needs. The report "Birth to 5 Matters" explains this further, suggesting that children become attached to significant adults who help the child feel safe, secure and valued (Early Years Coalition 2022).

The idea of a key person is to ensure that children have a network of adults who are attuned to their needs as well as provide a sense of belonging and supportive of their emotional well-being (Page, Clare and Nutbrown 2013). This means that when the child is not with their primary caregiver, then the key person in an early years setting will fulfil that role.

For children in primary and secondary schools, the Department for Education (DfE) produced statutory guidance for a designated teacher for CLA and children who are no longer in care but have care experiences (DfE 2018). The role of the designated teacher is not too different from that of the key person. They act as a central person who ensures the child's learning and development are promoted and disruption to the child is minimised. They are also seen to be the "safe" and consistent person for the CLA to go to in their times of need for support. Like the key person, the designated teacher is also responsible for the individual requirements of the child and to ensure that the CLA's time in school is tailored to meet their individual needs, promoting positive attachments to their teachers as well as valuing them as part of their school community. Grimmer (2021) explores the practitioners' role in promoting attachment, suggesting that they also provide a "safe haven" and a "secure base" where the child can rely on the practitioner for comfort as well as providing a solid foundation or environment that the child can explore. This is fundamental in the roles of both the key person and the designated teacher.

A key person and designated teacher are required for all CLA early years and educational practices, however, this does not end with allocating a professional to each child. The key person and designated teacher roles require professionals to apply strategies for building positive relationships and attachments with the CLA in their setting.

Some key strategies to build and maintain strong bonds of attachment with babies and children in practice include:

- Using positive body language, smiling at the child and being open to physical contact, such as holding hands or giving hugs.

- Using the child's name, making eye contact, and talking in a calm tone.
- Being able to respond quickly when a child is upset, validating their emotions, and supporting them sensitively.
- Knowing the child, being attuned to their cues, and recognising behavioural signs.
- Showing genuine interest in the child and their interests, providing opportunities to play together and plan activities around their interests.
- Spending one-on-one time with the child and giving them undivided attention.
- Chatting with the child generally throughout the day but also communicating routines with them.
- Praising their achievements.

These are actions which can be demonstrated daily with all the children in settings but specifically with those CLA and can easily be applied to the whole setting ethos and practice. These simple strategies allow the child to feel valued and have a sense of belonging within their environment. CLA will develop trust and a sense of security with those key and designated people who recognise and understand their needs and experiences of being CLA, and they will also thrive with those who invest a great deal of time and emotion in supporting their well-being and development (Page 2018).

But this does not end here, it is important as part of the role for professionals to demonstrate knowledge and understanding of attachment in both the long and short term when supporting children's holistic development (ECSDN 2020). A professional must be able to identify when a child is demonstrating specific attachment styles and try to help the child transition to having a secure attachment style.

Triangle of Love

Professionals should be able to promote an effective "triangle of love" while holding the child in mind (Page 2018: 129; Grimmer 2023: 2). This means that when building positive attachments with CLA, they should look to explore the relationships they also create with the child's primary caregiver. As mentioned previously, children who have a positive relationship with their caregivers will naturally follow their lead, they will read the interactions, body language and facial expressions of the caregiver whom they trust to decide if they are safe and secure. If they create positive relationships with the child's primary caregivers, children can perceive that the practitioner is someone to be trusted as their caregiver has demonstrated those signs of acceptance and trust (Hirst 2005). This can also work the opposite way; if a child has formed an anxious, avoidant, or disorganised attachment style, this will likely be displayed with the professional also, therefore making it harder to build those securely attached relationships. However, if the practitioner consistently applies some of the previously mentioned strategies, as well as patience and acceptance of the child, the child can learn to develop a secure attachment to the professional (Hughes 2018).

Trauma-Informed

CLA will struggle with the process of attaching to professionals significantly more than a child who has developed secure attachment. Therefore, it is important for professionals to be aware of the impact of their approach on children and what additional needs a CLA in this situation may have. A term that is commonly used to explain this is "trauma-informed". Professionals, where possible, should be informed of the trauma or potential trauma that a child may have experienced and use this information to help them build secure attachments in their setting. Not only this, but trauma-informed practice also helps put strategies in place so that children are not retraumatised and therefore can develop trusting relationships with those who care for them (Maynard et al. 2019). The key principle of trauma-informed practice is the creation of a safe environment; this can be done through demonstrating safety features to a child such as a secure building and safe spaces or through explaining setting rules and routines with the children, so they know what to expect (Cavanaugh 2016). This will mean that when the child experiences the rules and routines, they will trust what the professional has explained and what they have shown them will happen. Another strategy of being trauma-informed is positive interactions. Referring to the strategies identified earlier, these positive interactions suggest to the child that the professional is warm and welcoming, and a loving person who cares about them (Brown et al. 2022). A final key principle is creating culturally responsive practice, which means professionals should be responsive to the diversity of the children in their setting and acceptance of children's background and history (Cavanaugh 2016). This allows children to feel understood and validated while acknowledging the importance of a child's identity in forming relationship and others.

> *Reflective Questions*
>
> 1. What do you think you would do in your setting to support children who do not follow the usual pattern of attachment?
> 2. What strategies are there in your setting for promoting positive attachment?
> 3. Does your setting relate to the triangle of love or is it trauma-informed? What characteristics can you see of these in your setting?

Summary

Throughout this chapter, you have discussed different types of attachment styles and had an opportunity to see how these attachment styles can be demonstrated by CLA. The ACEs of CLA have been presented and we have shown how these can be a contributing factor to children's ability to form trusting, attached relationships with caregivers and practitioners. Alongside this you have had the opportunity to explore strategies for promoting positive attachment with practitioners and examples of how to do this in practice. Hopefully, this chapter has provided you with some food for thought about how to recognise signs of attachment difficulty for children and shown you how to develop your practice to promote attachment positively.

References

Association for Child and Adolescent Mental Health. (2020). Can We Improve Attachment or Attachment-Related Outcomes in Young Children? Available at: https://www.acamh.org/research-digest/can-improve-attachment-attachment-related-outcomes-young-children/

Beckes, L., Simons, K., Lewis, D., Le, A., and Edwards, W. (2021). Desperately Seeking Support: Negative Reinforcement Schedules in the Formation of Adult Attachment Associations. *Social Psychological & Personality Science*, 8(2), 229-238. DOI: 10.1177/1948550616671402

Boldt, L., Goffin, K., and Kochanska, G. (2020). The Significance of Early Parent-Child Attachment for Emerging Regulation: A Longitudinal Investigation of Processes and Mechanisms from Toddler Age to Preadolescence. *Developmental Psychology*, 56, 431-443. DOI: 10.1037/dev0000862

Bosmans, G., Verschueren, K., Cuyvers, B., and Minnis, H. (2020). Current Perspectives on the Management of Reactive Attachment Disorder in Early Education. *Psychology Research and Behavior Management*, 13, 1235-1246. DOI: 10.2147/PRBM.S264148

Bowlby, J. (1979). The Bowlby-Ainsworth Attachment Theory. *Behavioral and Brain Sciences*, 2(4), 637-638. DOI: 10.1017/S0140525X00064955

Brown, E.C., Freedle, A., Hurless, NL., Miller, R. D., Martin, C., and Paul, Z.A. (2022). Preparing Teacher Candidates for Trauma-Informed Practices. *Urban Education*, 57(4), 662-685. DOI: 10.1177/0042085920974084

Cahill, O., Holt, S., and Kirwan, G. (2016). Keyworking in Residential Child Care: Lessons from Research. *Children and Youth Services Review*, 65, 216-223. DOI: 10.1016/j.childyouth.2016.04.014

Cavanaugh, B. (2016). Trauma-Informed Classrooms and Schools. *Beyond Behavior*, 25(2), 41-46. Available at: http://www.jstor.org/stable/26381827

Cocker, C. and Allain, L. (2019). *Social Work with Looked After Children*. London: Learning Matters.

Collins, S. (2018). Embracing Cultural Responsivity and Social Justice: Re-Shaping Professional Identity in Counselling Psychology. *Canadian Journal of Counselling and Psychotherapy*, 55(2), 307-310. DOI: 10.47634/cjcp.v55i2.70579

DfE (Department for Education). (2014). Attachment Theory and Research. Available at: https://bjgp.org/content/bjgp/57/544/920.full.pdf

DfE (Department for Education). (2018). Designated Teacher For Looked-After And Previously Looked-After Children. Available at: https://www.gov.uk/government/publications/designated-teacher-for-looked-after-children

DfE (Department for Education). (2023). The Statutory Framework for the Early Years Foundation Stage. Available at: https://assets.publishing.service.gov.uk/government/uploads/system/uploads/attachment_data/file/974907/EYFS_framework_-_March_2023.pdf

DuPaul, G. J., Kern, L., Belk, G., Custer, B., Hatfield, A., Daffner, M., and Peek, D. (2018). Promoting Parent Engagement in Behavioral Intervention for Young Children with ADHD: Iterative Treatment Development. *Topics in Early Childhood Special Education*, 38(1), 42-53. DOI: 10.1177/0271121417746220

Early Years Coalition. (2022). Birth to 5 Matters: Attachment and the Role of the Key Person. Available at: https://birthto5matters.org.uk/attachment-and-the-role-of-the-key-person/

ECSDN. (2020). Early Childhood Graduate Practitioner Competencies. Available at: https://www.ecsdn.org/wp-content/uploads/2021/09/ECSDN-Booket-Rev-July-2020.pdf

Ellis, E. E., Yilanli, M., and Saadabadi, A. (2023). *Reactive Attachment Disorder*. In StatPearls [Internet]. Treasure Island (FL): StatPearls Publishing. Available at: https://www.ncbi.nlm.nih.gov/books/NBK537155/

Gillath, O. and Karantzas, G. (2019). Attachment Security Priming: A Systematic Review. *Current Opinion in Psychology*, 25, 86-95. DOI: 10.1016/j.copsyc.2018.03.001

Golmakani, N., Gholami, M., Shaghaghi, F., Safinejad, H., Kamali, Z., and Mohebbi-Dehnavi, Z. (2020). Relationship between Fear of Childbirth and the Sense of Cohesion with the Attachment of Pregnant Mothers to the Fetus. *Journal of Educational Health Promotion*, 30, 261. DOI: 10.4103/jehp.jehp_46_20. PMID: 33282966; PMCID: PMC7709774

Grimmer, T. (2021). *Developing a Loving Pedagogy in the Early Years*. Abingdon: Routledge.

Grimmer, T. (2023). Is There a Place for Love in an Early Childhood Setting? *Early Years*, 42(5), 1-14. DOI: 10.1080/09575146.2023.2182739

Hirst, M. (2005). *Loving and Living with Traumatised Children: Reflections by Adoptive Parents*. London: Coram BAAF.

Holmes, J. (2014). *John Bowlby and Attachment Theory*. 2nd edn. Abingdon: Routledge. https://doi.org/10.4324/9781315879772

Howe, D. (2017). *Child Abuse and Neglect: Attachment, Development and Intervention*. London: Bloomsbury.

Hughes, A. (2018). *Building the Bonds of Attachment*. 3rd edn. Lanham, MD: Rowman & Littlefield.

Katz, C., Tsur, N., Talmon. P., and Nicolet, R. (2021). Beyond Fight, Flight, and Freeze: Towards a New Conceptualization of Peritraumatic Responses to Child Sexual Abuse Based on Retrospective Accounts of Adult Survivors. *Child Abuse & Neglect*, 112. DOI: 10.1016/j.chiabu.2020.104905

Kobak, R. and Bosmans, G. (2019). Attachment and Psychopathology: A Dynamic Model of the Insecure Cycle. *Current Opinion in Psychology*, 25, 76-80. DOI: 10.1016/j.copsyc.2018.02.018

Lyu, X. (2023). A Literature Review of How Children Secure Attachment Predict Better Academic Performance. *Journal of Education, Humanities and Social Sciences*, 8, 1708-1714. DOI: 10.54097/ehss.v8i.4560

Mackin, J., Hillman, S., Cross, R., and Anderson, A. (2022). The Internal Worlds of Sexually Abused Looked-After Children. *The Psychoanalytic Study of the Child*, 75(1), 278-298. DOI: 10.1080/00797308.2021.2022413

Maynard, B.R., Farina, A., Dell, N.A., and Kelly, M.S. (2019). Effects of Trauma-Informed Approaches in Schools: A Systematic Review. *Campbell Systematic Reviews*, 15(1), 1-2.

McBlain, S. (2022). *Learning Theories for Early Years Practice*. 2nd edn. London: Sage.

Murphy, R., Goodall, K., and Woodrow, A. (2020). The Relationship Between Attachment Insecurity and Experiences on the Paranoia Continuum: A Meta-Analysis. *The British Journal of Clinical Psychology*, 59(3), 290-318. DOI: 10.1111/bjc.12247

Neaum, S. (2022). *Child Development for Early Years Students and Practitioners*. 5th edn. London: Sage.

NICE (National Institute for Health and Care Excellence). (2021). *Looked After Children and Young People*. Available at: https://www.nice.org.uk/guidance/NG205

NSPCC (National Society for the Prevention of the Cruelty to Children). (2023). *Attachment and Child Development*. Available at: https://learning.nspcc.org.uk/child-health-development/attachment-early-years

O'Connor, A. (2017). *Understanding Transitions in the Early Years: Supporting Change through Attachment and Resilience*. 2nd edn. Abingdon: Routledge.

Page, J. (2018). Characterising the Principles of Professional Love in Early Childhood Care and Education. *International Journal of Early Years Education*, 26(2), 125-141. DOI: 10.1080/09669760.2018.1459508

Page, J., Clare, A., and Nutbrown, K. (2013). *Working with Babies & Children: Birth to Three*. 2nd edn. London: Sage.

Pallini, S., Morellib, M., Chirumbolob, A., Baioccob, R., Laghib, F. and Eisenberg, N. (2019). Attachment and Attention Problems: A Meta-Analysis. *Clinical Psychology Review*, 74. DOI: 10.1016/j.cpr.2019.101772

Partridge, O., Maguire, T., and Newman-Taylor, K. (2022). How Does Attachment Style Affect Psychosis? A Systematic Review of Causal Mechanisms and Guide to Future Inquiry. *Psychology and Psychotherapy*, 95(1), 345-380. DOI: 10.1111/papt.12371

Raby, K.L. and Dozier, M. (2019). Attachment Across the Lifespan: Insights from Adoptive Families. *Current Opinion in Psychology*, 25, 81-85.

Rees, C. (2007). Childhood Attachment. *British Journal of Practice*, 57(544), 920-922.

Skinner, E. and Wellborn, J. (2019). *Coping During Childhood and Adolescence: A Motivational Perspective*. Abingdon: Routledge.

Smith, M., Cameron, C., and Reimer, D. (2017). From Attachment to Recognition for Children in Care. *The British Journal of Social Work*, 47(6), 1606-1623. DOI: 10.1093/bjsw/bcx096

Sroufe, A. (2016). *Attachment Theory: A Humanistic Approach for Research and Practice Across Cultures*. London: Routledge.

Sroufe, A. (2021). Then and Now: The Legacy and Future of Attachment Research. *Attachment & Human Development*, 23, 1-8. DOI: 10.1080/14616734.2021.1918450

Strand, P.S., Vossen, J.J., and Savage, E. (2019). Culture and Child Attachment Patterns: A Behavioral Systems Synthesis. *Perspectives in Behavioural Sciences*, 42, 835-850. DOI: 10.1007/s40614-019-00220-3

Wardecker, B.M., Chopik, W.J., Moors, A.C., and Edelstein, R.S. (2020). Avoidant Attachment Style. In *Encyclopedia of Personality and Individual Differences*. Cham: Springer International Publishing, pp. 345-351.

Wurster, H. and Biringen, Z. (2023). Validity of the Emotional Attachment Zones Evaluation (EA-Z): Assessing Attachment Style Across a Developmental Spectrum. *Perspectives on Early Childhood Psychology and Education*, 5(1). Available at: https://digitalcommons.pace.edu/perspectives/vol5/iss1/1

6
Who Are My Family and What Do They Do?

CHAPTER AIMS

This chapter will explore the family unit and some of the reasons why children become children looked after. We will look at the importance of family in children's development and how this influences children socially. By the end of this chapter, you will be able to do the following:

- Understand the impact of family on Children Looked After (CLA) and how this influences children's development.
- Explore different family dynamics and the role of the immediate and extended family.
- Examine different placements and "home" environments for children in care.
- Review the importance of birth family and sibling contact for CLA.

Keywords

care, family, foster, placements

Introduction

This chapter will explore the different types of family dynamics and the impact the family has on Children Looked After (CLA). The family is extremely important to all children, in instilling values, beliefs and social stability. Not only this, but families help children make decisions, support the development of self-esteem as well as nurturing and protecting children. For CLA, the family plays an important role in their lives. CLA, as identified in Chapter 1, have been removed from the family home and are living in the care of others, be it foster families, in kinship care or other forms of local authority placement. The impact of this is reviewed throughout this book, however, in this chapter, we will explore the different types of families and living arrangements for children and how this is perceived by society but also by the children themselves. We will begin with what it means to be a family.

What Is a Family?

By definition, a family is a group of one or more parents living together with their children (*Cambridge English Dictionary* 2024). For many, a family is a secure unit of people who have a shared interest in each other but also care and look after each other. In most families, parents will care for the children and have the responsibility of keeping the children safe and protected, ensuring their needs are met to help them thrive and develop. Families, not only meet children's basic survival needs, but also provide love, support, and encouragement to help children feel loved, valued and belong within their network of people. Families are often seen as a child's biggest supporters and advocates.

Durkheim ([1895] 1982) proposes functionalism, a sociological theory which interprets how a family functions in society today. According to functionalism, the family in society today performs five functions which are vital in contributing to the overall well-being and functioning of individuals and the larger community. Figure 6.1 is a breakdown of Durkheim's five family functions in society.

Figure 6.1 shows that the family is crucial in supporting children to develop both emotionally and socially. The family is responsible for teaching children the morals of society and helping mould their sense of identity and shaping how they are portrayed to the community

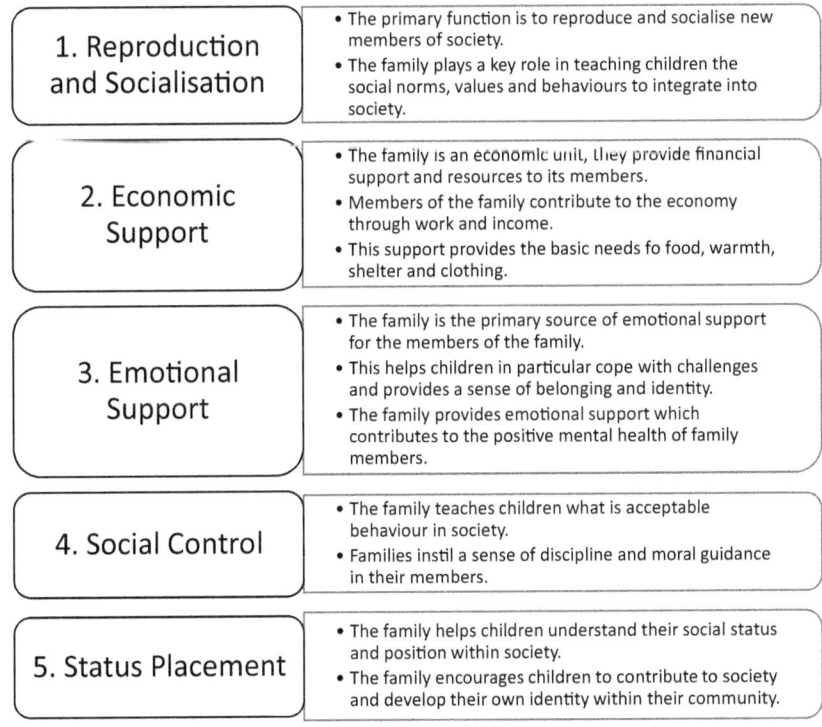

Figure 6.1 Durkheim's five functions of the family in society

Source: Edwards (2024).

76 Advocating for Children Looked After

but also how they view themselves (Brock 2023). Where a child is from a strong, connected and stable family, these functions are deemed as positive and children will develop a strong sense of self, based on who their family is and how they have been brought up and cared for (Smith 2020). However, for CLA, for children who have not had these positive experiences, the functions of the family identified by Durkheim, the family will not have positively impacted the child. Therefore, a CLA may not have the same morals and beliefs, interpretation of right and wrong, have experienced positive emotional support or even experienced shelter, food and warmth and therefore this will affect how the child is viewed and perceived in society when they are unable to conform to the social norms. Durkheim ([1895] 1982) believed that children who have not experienced a "rational morality", a sense of widely accepted right and wrong, cannot develop positive relationships within society in the same way as others who have experienced this.

The Importance of Family

According to Durkheim's theory of functionalism, the family plays an important role for children in society. But how else do families influence children? Bronfenbrenner (1979, cited in Grimmer 2022) stated that people do not live in isolation, they are part of a network or community and belong to families. Bronfenbrenner identified this network of people as the ecological system: microsystem, mesosystem, exosystem, macrosystem, and chronosystem (Figure 6.2). He believed that the environment in which a child grows up will have a great impact on a child's development and the people who engage with children have a role in shaping how a child will develop. Bronfenbrenner (1979, cited in Bradbury and Swailes 2022) identified five systems which reflect the different levels of impact on children. The closer the system is to the child, the more influence these will have on the child. The focus is on the child and all systems have the child as the centre of their priorities.

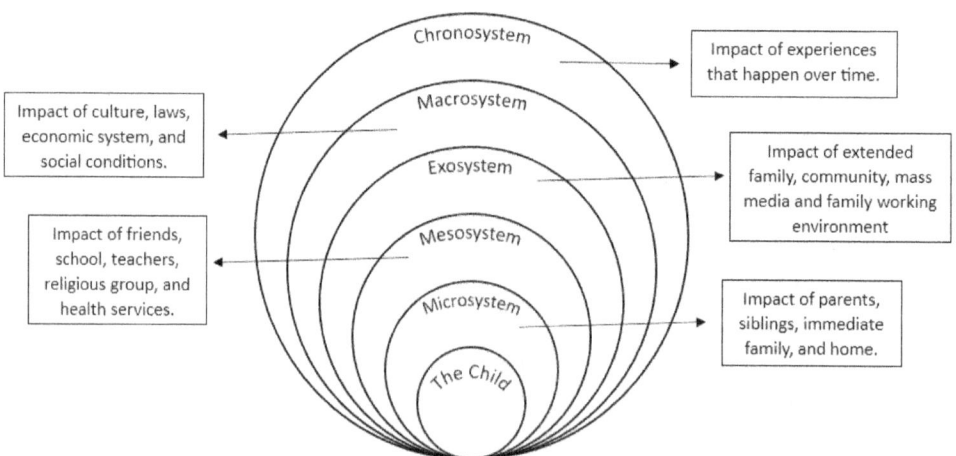

Figure 6.2 Bronfenbrenner's ecological systems

> In order to develop normally, a child requires progressively more complex joint activity with one or more adults who have an irrational emotional relationship with the child. Somebody's got to be crazy about that kid. That's number one. First, last and always.
>
> (Bronfenbrenner 1979)

However, for CLA, their immediate microsystem (family) is likely not to have had adults around them who are irrationally crazy about that child. As explored in Chapters 1 and 4, to be in care, the child will have experienced a lack of loving supportive families, a lack of positive role models and evidence of their physical and emotional needs not being met. This will have a direct impact on a child's development and future outcomes. The identified adverse experiences within the microsystem will consequently affect the systems following this. Chapter 5 delves deeply into the significance of attachment in children's future development, with Bowlby (1979) stating: "If a community values its children, it must cherish their parents." The community (the mesosystem and beyond) will place value on the child and provide resources for the child based on the circumstances which the child has found themselves. Therefore, a CLA who has had little value placed on them by the parents and family will feel the effects of this as they move through society and will naturally be treated differently in society due to their known family history. Like any other child, CLA will learn and develop their identity based on the community of people who surround them. They will pick up and mimic behaviours and traits from their parents, siblings and other primary people in their lives and will use these as a way of interpreting and navigating through social situations. This means that for a child who may have been surrounded by negativity or not experience the love and support we would expect from a family, this can have dramatic impacts on how they behave in different situations but also how they show love and affection to others in their lives. The further one moves through the ecological systems, the less impact is had on the formation of the child's life and development, but these systems still have the potential to influence the child significantly. For example, CLA will have regular contact with a social worker. Typically, according to Bronfenbrenner's ecological system (1971, cited in Bradbury and Grimmer 2024), social workers sit in the exosystem or macrosystem area. However, for CLA, social workers will be making the important choices and decisions for their well-being and therefore play a much greater role. It could be argued that in the case of CLA, the social worker becomes part of the child's microsystem. However, Thomas and Winter (2024) argue that despite the social worker having parental responsibilities for the child, this does not replace the child's need for a loving and stable microsystem which cannot be provided within the professional role of the social worker.

For CLA, it is important for them to have a sense of belonging and be part of a community, which loves, values and supports them. As identified in Chapter 1, this helps to secure their identity and understanding of who they are and the type of person they want to be. Thomas and Winter (2024) argue that in the case of CLA, the school, the professionals and their peers with whom they have consistent and positive interactions can have a significantly greater impact on the child, especially supporting them to navigate and understand the adversity they have experienced. Professionals, such as teachers, pastoral teams within schools and social workers, may often be the only consistent figures that a child may encounter, and these professionals often replace the traditional role model for children that parents fill in the lives of average children. Warrington et al. (2023) argue that the role of the professionals for CLA is to provide reassurance, support and the possibility of belonging to the community of people in which they find themselves. For example, teachers help children to feel accepted in their school community, and social workers will support children to feel settled and belong within their foster placements and social community. These different communities have an important influence not only on the child's identity development but also on their social, emotional and cognitive development. As discussed in Chapter 1, if the child feels safe, secure and that they belong, they have more opportunity and likelihood of succeeding in the future.

Peers and friends play an important role in the lives of all children, however, for CLA, we have seen that the process of making friends and feeling accepted within their groups of peers is often difficult, as they have significant differences in upbringing and background. CLA often feel embarrassed to share their stories as this opens them up to criticism and bullying, stemming from other children not understanding their circumstances and being unable to relate to what the child has experienced. We have also explored that children who have not experienced positive role models and loving homes have difficulty forming and maintaining relationships (Collins 2018). This applies not only to the role of the child and caregiver but also to the child and their peers. After experiencing adverse childhood experiences (ACEs) children often find it difficult to trust others, and to share their experiences but also suffer fear of others not understanding them. According to Lee-Brindle (2018), peers play a massive role in the social identity of the child but also support CLA to understand different social contexts and adapt their behaviour to "fit in" to different situations and environments. Peers also often understand the complex ways of thinking that a child may be experiencing, as they do have experience of the pressures from society and the community. Through mutual interests and a willingness to understand the differences between them, peers play a crucial role in helping the child to trust others but also develop an understanding of themselves and the type of person that they want to be (Lee-Brindle 2018).

What Do Families Look Like?

Over time, families have developed and come in all shapes and sizes, made up of different people. Within families, people play various roles to support the family and the children. Here we will summarise the different types of families in society today before looking at different types of families for CLA.

Nuclear or Traditional Family

The image of family that most people see when they think of a family is the traditional or nuclear family (Figure 6.3). A nuclear family is made up of two parents and children. Throughout history, it was traditional for the women or mothers of the family to stay at home and care for the children while the males or fathers worked. This traditional family make-up has evolved through time and traditionally now it can be seen that the family roles are much more equal between the parents, with both supporting the family through work and also sharing responsibilities with childcare. We have also seen that nuclear families are no longer confined to gender roles of men and women but present more diversity in how the nuclear family is made up, meaning that parents who are of the same gender and sexual orientation are included within the definition of nuclear families as long as there are two parents.

Single-Parent Family

A single-parent family is one parent living with one or more children (Figure 6.4). It may be that the parents have separated, forming two single-parent families or a parent may be the only parent that the child has, through death, separation or no involvement from the other parent. A family may also be a single-parent family through choice, with the parent having made the decision to raise their child alone, having no identified partner.

Extended family

The extended family has two or more generations living in the same house. Typically, this would be grandparents living with parents and children, but it is not uncommon for aunts, uncles, or cousins to live in the same home (Figure 6.5). There could be several reasons for families to live with their extended family members, but it is usually because relatives within the family need additional care and support. This could be due to health, disability, or age or even to support family members with childcare and living costs.

Stepfamilies

Stepfamilies or blended families are when one or both of the child's parents have established new relationships with another partner who is not the child's primary parent (Figure 6.6). The child may acquire stepsiblings either through their stepparent already having children or new children being born into the family by their stepparent and parent.

Kinship Families

This is when another member of the extended family cares for the child instead of their parents (See Figure 6.7). This could be due to the parent's inability to care for their child, or they could have died, leaving the child to be cared for by another relative, such as a grandparent, aunts or uncles.

CLA may have begun life in or developed into one of the above types of family structures. However, when a child goes into the care of the local authority, this image of family may look extremely different. For some children, they can be under the parental responsibility of the local authority but may be cared for by kinship carers. In this instance, the family image would be very similar to the above kinship family. However, the difference is that the local authority will make the overall decisions regarding the child, keeping the best interests of the child in mind. Kinship carers are good for CLA as they allow the child to still feel a sense of belonging and strong links to their heritage and family ties. They may still have contact with their birth parents and kinship carers can help children understand who they are and where they have come from, as well as maintain some positive, attached relationships with people who are known to them.

Living Arrangements for CLA

Now we will explore the different types of living arrangements for children who are in care.

Foster Families

Foster families or foster placements, as they are sometimes referred to, are a family or even an individual foster parent or foster carer looking after a child who has been placed into care by the local authority (Figure 6.8). The foster carer will have been approved by the social team within the local authority as a safe and suitable person for the child to live with. They will have completed specific training to become a foster carer as well as going through rigorous checks to ensure that they are prepared to support the needs of CLA. The foster carer or family will be expected to meet the needs of the child, provide them with a stable and loving home environment and support them to thrive in the home environment. In return for doing this, the foster carer or family receive a wage from the local authority. Foster families are important for CLA as they will be the people with whom CLA spend the most time and hopefully they will develop positive relationships and attachments with their foster carers. When children develop positive relationships with their foster families, they do well socially, emotionally, and cognitively but this also allows the child to experience a positive family life and allows them to feel a sense of belonging and support to overcome the impact of the adversity they have experienced. Although moving a child to a foster family is always in the best interest of the child, this move is often difficult at first as the child likely does not know the foster carers and their family and may have difficulty trusting them and fitting into their family life. However, Naish (2018) suggests that with proper support from social workers and other therapeutic professionals, children will be able to become more settled and accustomed to life with a foster family, especially with experienced foster carers.

Respite Foster Carers

A CLA may come to live, for a short period of time, with respite foster carers (Figure 6.9). This is usually when the child's regular foster carer needs a break, a holiday or some time away from caring for the child. The respite foster carers or family will fulfil the usual role of the foster carer, ensuring that the needs of the child are being met and that the child is thriving. The child's social worker maintains responsibility for the child while they are with respite foster carers and will ensure that the respite foster carer is suitable to meet the child's needs. It may be that the respite foster carer knows the child or has had some transition sessions in
the lead-up to the respite care. Respite carers will have had the same security checks and training to properly equip them to support CLA but also will have experience of caring for CLA for short periods of time as children doing short placement moves are likely to be more unsettled as they have developed attachment to their foster carer.

Emergency Foster Carers

Emergency foster carers and families are contacted in cases of emergency to care for children (Figure 6.10). Cases of emergency vary, however, the most common is that a child has been removed from their family home or living situation and a safe place for the child to stay and live is the priority of the authorities. For example, if the police find children to be living in an unsafe environment or the child's primary carers are being arrested with no other known family to care for the child, social services within the local authority will seek an emergency foster carer for the child to go to. Emergency foster carers look after children on an extremely temporary

basis while a more permanent living situation is identified or if it is decided that the child can go back to their previous carers. Emergency foster carers like foster carers and respite foster carers will have completed the relevant security checks and training to support and care for children in this way and will have also been identified as the most suitable option for the child in the identified state of emergency.

Adoptive Families

As discussed in Chapter 1, a child who is unable to return to their primary caregivers or parents, for whatever reason, will go through the courts and the child's allocated social worker from the local authority will apply for a placement order. This means that the child requires a permanent home and family. For adoptive families (Figure 6.11), the process of adoption can take many months as the families are thoroughly checked to ensure that they can offer a safe and secure home to the child. The physical home as well as the emotional and social network of the family and those expected to live with the child will be investigated to ensure their suitability for caring and loving the child as their own. It is also important that the potential adoptive family are identified as being able to financially support the child, as when a child is adopted, they are legally a member of the family and perceived as if they have been born into the family, meaning that there is no financial gain or regular income from adopting a child as there is if the family became foster carers. It is important for adoptive families to undergo training to prepare themselves for the potential needs that a CLA may have, but also so they are the best people to support the child, following the adversity they have experienced. Adoptive families are seen as the best way to offer children a stable, secure, and loving home life, which will help them develop positively for the rest of their lives and have the opportunity to experience a happy home environment. Despite children no longer being considered in care when they are adopted, they are referred to as care leavers, and therefore still carry the label of being in care which, as discussed in Chapter 2, carries significant weight for the child.

Family Relationships for CLA

As discussed, CLA will have contact with different types of families in their lives, however, just because a CLA is living with a foster family does not mean that contact with their birth families will end. How this is facilitated and supported positively needs careful consideration from professionals so that children can benefit from the relationships they are maintaining. In this next section of the chapter, we will review what the relationships for CLA will look like with their siblings and also their birth parents.

Sibling Relationships

Wherever possible, professionals will do their best to keep families together. Where a child has been placed in local authority care, social workers and family professionals will try to keep siblings together and place them with the same foster families (Figure 6.12). This is beneficial for children as they have  experienced the trauma of going to care together, they have shared understanding of the circumstances which bond them together but, more importantly, they are part of each other's identity and history. CLA have special connections with their siblings and often feel that no one else in the world can understand their individual circumstances other than their sibling. It is also believed, that when a lack of consistent, loving parental figures has been identified, a sibling will often replace the role of important caregiver, with CLA often looking after each other and prioritising their sibling's needs over their own, which one would usually expect a parent to do. Not all siblings have a close relationship, however, having a sibling present can provide a trusted person with whom to share their anxieties. They can also provide a point of familiarity in the midst of so much that seems strange and foreign to the CLA. It is therefore important for all professionals to consider all possibilities for keeping siblings together to ensure that these positive relationships are maintained, and children do not incur further trauma of being separated. Research conducted by the Children's Commissioner (2023) states that siblings who remain together have better long-term outcomes and thrive better in their lives within the foster family.

In some cases, it is simply not possible for siblings to remain together in care. There could be several reasons for this, the main one being that a suitable placement cannot be sourced to accommodate the children, for example, a foster family may not be available to care for a large number of children. Another main reason could be that it is in the best interests of the children to be separated in order to fulfil the long-term needs of the children. Where separation happens, it is done as the very last option for social workers and will only be done following a sibling assessment, which is usually conducted by a therapist who is trained and experienced in childhood trauma. It is only at the recommendation of the professionals and in the complete best interests of the individual siblings for them to be separated from each other.

To minimise the impact and further trauma of another family separation, it is the job of professionals to ensure that positive contact is established and maintained between the siblings. Where siblings can build and maintain positive, lasting relationships with each other, it can have a significant positive impact on their social and emotional development as well as the ability to continue to build and maintain attached relationships with others in the future (McWey, Cui and Wojciak 2023). Having positive sibling contact is widely recognised as being beneficial to CLA's happiness and plays an important role in developing and maintaining self-esteem, identity, permanence, and love. Maintaining sibling contact in care comes with many challenges which the next section of this chapter explores.

Challenges for maintaining sibling contact

As discussed, when separated in care, siblings need to maintain contact with each other to effectively promote their long-term outcomes, and also this allows the child to maintain a sense of self and their identity. However, it can often be challenging for professionals, practitioners and the children to have contact with their siblings. The key challenges that are faced when promoting contact between siblings are shown in Figure 6.13.

Lack of Support	Legal Constraints	Emotional Impact	Age Differences	Communication Challenges
•Caregivers, social workers and other professionals may not prioritise or actively facilitate sibling contact. •This can lead to missed opportunities to strengthen and maintain sibling relationships.	•Legal restrictions or concerns about the safety of individual CLA can limit contact. •This is significant where there is a history or abuse or contact is deemed unsafe to maintain.	•Siblings may experience feelings of loss, longing or frustration when they cannot see each other regularly. •This may cause the CLA to behave negatively when around professionals, especially those they feel are responsible for the separation.	•Age gaps can affect the nature of sibling relationships. •Maintaining contact can be difficult or finding common ground or shared interests where there is a large gap in age.	•Siblings may struggle with communication barriers. •It is not uncommon for children to have developed different communication styles and emotional needs. •This makes communicating effectively with siblings difficult as they are striving to be heard.

Figure 6.13 Key challenges for CLA with sibling contact

Reflective Questions

1. Which challenges do you think would impact siblings' relationship the most?
2. How can professionals try to navigate and overcome some of these challenges to promote effective contact between siblings?

Birth Family Contact

We must remember that not all children become looked after permanently, sometimes they are in care until the child's parents can evidence that they can provide a secure and loving home for the child. CLA may at some point return to their birth families or they may remain in care until they turn 18. Therefore, while they are in care, they can have contact with their birth families and siblings (Figure 6.14). This contact is organised formally through the child's social worker and is often conducted in a safe environment such as an approved contact centre or public place where the child's foster carer and/or social worker can attend to supervise the contact. These arrangements are supported by the Children Act (1989) and require professionals in local authorities to support CLA's contact with birth families, unless it is not in the best interest of the child, in which the case for a non-contact order will be justified and approved by the courts. A non-contact order would be issued in cases where children are severely traumatised and likely to have negative responses to having contact with the birth family. Continued and positive contact with a child's birth family provides continuity for CLA, most of whom will have experienced multiple losses during their lives. Not only this, but birth family contact also provides CLA with links to their identity, culture and background, children will know where they come from, and the birth family will be able to continue to support the child with understanding their experiences and how they came to be in care. Not only does this benefit the child, but this type of contact also benefits the birth parents. It allows them to feel reassured that the child is being well cared for and they are not forgotten. This perspective is also shared by the child, who often will worry about their family but through contact they can be reassured that they are safe and have not forgotten them.

Challenges to Birth Family Contact

Many foster families report challenges following their foster child having contact with their birth families. It is important that, as professionals supporting CLA, we are aware of these challenges but also we must be able to offer support to both the foster families and children to have a more positive experience following their birth family contact. Figure 6.15 presents some of the identified challenges children may encounter with birth family contact:

Changes in behaviour	Heightened emotional state	Regresssion and breakdown in relationship
• Seeing birth families can bring difficult memories to the forefront. • When returning to their foster family, it is a stark reminder of their circumstances and how they came to be in care. • Children often demonstrate regressive behaviour, they may show aggression or signs of social and emotional irregularity.	• Children can have feelings of loss, rejection and sadness following a visit with their birth family. • Children may demonstrate heightened emotional reactions to normal situations within their environment. • They may be inconsolable, clingy and seeking extreme closeness and comfort from their foster carer.	• Following contact with birth families, children may regress in their attachment and show distance from their foster families. • Out of loyalty to their birth families, children may show negativity towards their foster carers as a sign of not wanting to get too close to them or replace their parental figures. • This can make it difficult for foster carers to bring their relationship with the child back to a place of positivity.

Figure 6.15 Birth family contact challenges

86 Advocating for Children Looked After

> *Reflective Questions*
>
> 1. Which challenges do you think would impact the child's relationships the most?
> 2. How can professionals try to navigate and overcome some of these challenges to promote effective contact between birth families and foster carers?
> 3. How do we prepare children for contact between siblings and birth families?

What Do We Do?

This is a tricky question to answer, as has become clear throughout the other chapters in this book, no two children experience their trauma and adversity in the same way with the same outcomes. This, therefore, can also be said about family contact, no two children will react the same when faced with contact between birth family and siblings. But what we can do is try and prepare the child and the families as best we can. This comes with challenges, but we can look to navigate these and prepare for all different situations. Figure 6.16 presents some possible strategies we can apply to help children feel more settled when approaching contact with birth families and siblings.

In preparation for CLA to have contact with their birth families and siblings, we also need to consider the support and strategies which can be applied to help prepare foster families and professionals for these visits. Figure 6.17 presents some strategies for foster families and professionals to prepare for contact

> *Reflective Questions*
>
> 1. What challenges do you think you might face when supporting the child in a visit with their siblings and birth families?
> 2. Do you feel confident that you could encourage positive engagement from the child and their families?
> 3. What would this positive encouragement look like and how would the child, the foster families and birth families feel about this?

Some children will like to know the dates in advance to feel prepared.	Some children prefer not to know when it is happening to avoid disappointment if the contact does not happen.	Support children to explore their wishes and desires from the contact. For young children, this could be as simple as playing on the swings, for older children, it could be having difficult conversations.
Being open and honest about the contact and the expectations of the contact.	Discuss with the child the possibility of the contact not going ahead and what will happen if someone does not attend.	Make arrangements for safe words or objects to be used if the child is uncomfortable and wants to end the contact early. This allows the child safely to know that they do not have to force the contact if they are unhappy.

Figure 6.16 Strategies for preparing children for birth family and sibling contact

Help the foster family to identify a safe place for the child to return to after the contact.	It is important not to be judgemental or criticise the birth family and siblings. This may lead to the child feeling they need to choose between the foster family and their birth families.	Find ways to help the child settle and regulate following the visit. Allow the child space to express their feelings, and offer comfort to them. Also do not be offended if the child rejects the foster family. The child may need time to process their feelings.
	Children thrive on regular routine, where possible, encourage contact to be arranged around the child's normal routine but also allow consistent contact arrangements to be made.	Ensure you, as the professional responsible for the child, consider the child's needs and feelings. Make judgements on what is best for the child, even if it is difficult for the foster family.

Figure 6.17 Strategies for overcoming challenges with birth family and sibling contact

Summary

In this chapter, we have brought together concepts from the earlier chapters to gain an understanding of children's families and the importance of family on CLA's well-being and development. We explored the different types of family structures and characteristics of these different living arrangements. We acknowledge the importance of CLA maintaining consistent and positive contact with their birth families and siblings but also the challenges that we professionals may face when promoting birth family and sibling contact. It is important to remember the value of family on children's identity and sense of self and, despite our knowledge and feelings towards the child's birth family, where possible, positive relationships must be encouraged and supported to the benefit of the child.

References

Bowlby, J. (1979). The Bowlby-Ainsworth Attachment Theory. *Behavioral and Brain Sciences*, 2(4), 637–638.
Bradbury, A. and Grimmer, T. (2024) *Love & Nurture in Early Years*. London: Learning Matters.
Bradbury, A. and Swailes, R. (eds) (2022). *Early Childhood Theories Today*. London: Sage Publications.
Bronfenbrenner U. (1979). *The Ecology of Human Development: Experiments by Nature and Design*. Cambridge, MA: Harvard University Press.
Brock, T. (2023). *Social Theory*. London: Sage.
Cambridge English Dictionary (2024). Cambridge: Cambridge University Press.
Children's Commissioner. (2023). Siblings in Care. Available at: https://assets.childrenscommissioner.gov.uk/wpuploads/2023/01/cc-siblings-in-care.pdf
Collins, S. (2018). Ethics of Care and Statutory Social Work in the UK: Critical Perspectives And Strengths. *Practice*, 30(1), 3–18.
Durkheim, E. ([1895] 1982). *The Rules of Sociological Method and Selected Texts on Sociology and Its Method* (ed. S. Lukes, trans. W. D. Halls). New York: The Free Press.
Edwards, M. (2024). The Functionalist View of Family in Sociology. Available at: https://easysociology.com/sociology-of-family-relationships/the-functionalist-view-of-family-in-sociology/#:~:text=The%20Functions%20of%20Family%201%201.%20Reproduction%20and,Social%20Control%20...%205%205.%20Status%20Placement%20

Grimmer, T. (2022) Urie Bronfenbrenner. In A. Bradbury, and R. Swailes (eds), *Early Childhood Theories Today*. London: Sage Publications.

Lee-Brindle, G.F. (2018). Understanding Looked After Children's Experience with Peers: An Exploration of Young People's Social Understanding of Children in Care (Doctoral dissertation, University of Surrey).

McWey, L.M., Cui, M., and Wojciak, A.S. (2023). The Importance of Sibling Relationships in Buffering Against Depressive Symptoms of Youth in Foster Care. *Families in Society*, 104(4), 465-475.

Naish, S. (2018) *The A-Z of Therapeutic Parenting: Strategies and Solutions*. London: Jessica Kingsley Publishers

Smith, P. (2020). *Durkheim and After*. London: Polity Press.

Thomas, N.P. and Winter, K. (2024). *Social Work with Young People In Care: Looking After Children in Theory and Practice*. London: Routledge.

Warrington, C., Beckett, H., Allnock, D., and Soares, C. (2023). Children's Perspectives on Family Members' Needs and Support After Child Sexual Abuse. *Children and Youth Services Review*, 149, 106925.

7
Government Agenda

CHAPTER AIMS

In this chapter, we will examine, through legislation, policy and guidance what the government views are on Children Looked After (CLA), care-experienced children and care leavers and what the government are doing to support children, young people and their families. By the end of this chapter, you will be able to do the following:

- Examine legislation, policy and guidance documents that are intended to support CLA, children who are care experienced and care leavers.
- Acknowledge the role of multi-agency collaboration when supporting the educational outcomes of CLA or children who are care experienced.
- Be aware of the use of government funding to raise attainment and support for care leavers.
- Explore the effectiveness of the reforms to children's social care in England.

Keywords

care leavers, Early Years Foundation Stage, Early Years Pupil Premium, legislation, National Curriculum, Pupil Premium Plus, Pupil Premium, safeguarding, statutory guidance

Introduction

The Department for Education (DfE 2023a) claims that 400,000 children are supported every day by local authority social care services and that there are approximately five children in every classroom in England who have been supported by a social worker. We will discuss in Chapter 9 why CLA or care-experienced children are at a higher risk of having poorer educational outcomes, along with what strategies and interventions can be implemented to support children to achieve their full potential. However, it is also important to examine and understand what the statutory requirements are when supporting CLA or children who are care experienced so we can deliver high-quality provision where it is needed the most.

DOI: 10.4324/9781032716978-7

Table 7.1 Definitions of terms

Term	Definition
Legislation	Sets out the law
Policy	• Is a set of ideas, plans or courses of action. A 'government policy' is a statement about the government's position, intent or action. • is overarching statements that organisations use to guide their practice, so the law is followed. Policies must always comply with existing law.
Procedure	Outlines the specific steps and actions needed to be taken for organisations to follow a policy
Guidance	Guidance and advice is more than likely to be based on legislation and will offer the appropriate ways to make sure the law is being followed.

A society's underlying beliefs and values can be shown through its laws, policies, guidelines, and strategies. As a result of examining these, we can gain a clear understanding of the government's perception of the most vulnerable groups in our society. We can also learn what they are doing to improve the outcomes for CLA. Before we continue, it is useful to understand what the common terms and definitions are when referring to various laws, government policies and guidance (Table 7.1).

Legislation

The legislative Acts outlined in Table 7.2 are a few of the main pieces of legislation that have statutory implications for CLA and care leavers. It is important to see how legislation has developed since the Children Act 1989 and how the government at that time acknowledged the support and resources that CLA needed.

Education and Curriculum

As part of the Early Years Foundation Stage (EYFS) and the National Curriculum, standards are set for learning as well as for the care and welfare of children. As all children, including CLA, will spend most of their time in education, it is essential that we examine how the curricula in England support the needs of CLA so they are able to reach their full academic potential.

Early Years Foundation Stage

The Early Years Foundation Stage (EYFS; DfE 2023b) is a statutory requirement that sets the standards for the learning, development and care of children from birth to 5 years old. All schools and Ofsted-registered provisions such as childminders, nurseries and preschools are required to follow the EYFS. To be used in conjunction with the EYFS, non-statutory guidance, such as Development Matters (DfE 2023c) or Birth to 5 Matters (Early Years Coalition 2023), supports practitioners in following the requirements identified in the EYFS (DfE 2023c).

Table 7.2 Timeline and overview of government legislation

Acts of Parliament	A brief overview of some of the key principles
Children Act 1989 https://www.legislation.gov.uk/ukpga/1989/41/contents	The concept of parental responsibility The child's welfare is paramount Children are best looked after by their families unless deemed unsafe The duty placed on local authorities to promote and safeguard the child's welfare
Children (Leaving Care) Act 2000 https://www.legislation.gov.uk/ukpga/2000/35/notes/division/2	Arrangements for financial support for care leavers are much simpler Helps care leavers move from care to living independently
Adoption and Children Act 2002 https://www.legislation.gov.uk/ukpga/2002/38/notes/division/2	Aligns with the Children Act 1989 to ensure the child's welfare is paramount Duties placed on local authorities to maintain adoption service and assessment of needs Adoption orders to be made in favour of single people, married and unmarried couples
Children Act 2004 https://www.legislation.gov.uk/ukpga/1989/41/contents	Amendment to Children Act 1989 Duties placed on all agencies working with children and their families to ensure the need for safeguarding and promotion of welfare is the main consideration in their practice
Education and Inspections Act 2006 https://www.legislation.gov.uk/ukpga/2006/40/contents	Ensures that children get the education they need to fulfil their potential Increases diversity and devolves responsibility to schools by introducing Trusts Fairer access to schools Reforms of the National Curriculum and introduction of specialised diplomas Statutory right for school staff to discipline children New nutritional standards for food and drink in maintained schools
Children and Families Act 2014 https://www.legislation.gov.uk/ukpga/2014/6/contents t 2014	Introduces a wide range of policies from different government departments to improve services for key groups of vulnerable children and to support families Reduces barriers to adoption Reforms the family justice system Places children at the centre of decision-making Wider childcare issues such as shared parental leave
Children and Social Work Act 2017 https://www.legislation.gov.uk/ukpga/2017/16/contents/enacted	Establishes local arrangements for safeguarding and promoting children's welfare Introduction of three safeguarding partners: local authority, NHS Integrated Care Boards and police forces

> **OVERVIEW OF THE STRUCTURE OF THE EARLY YEARS FOUNDATION STAGE**
>
> *Seven key features of effective practice*
>
> 1. The best for every child
> 2. High-quality care
> 3. The curriculum: what we want children to learn
> 4. Pedagogy: helping children to learn
> 5. Assessment: checking what children have learnt
> 6. Self-regulation and executive function
> 7. Partnership with parents
>
> *Characteristics of effective teaching and learning*
>
> 1. Playing and exploring
> 2. Active learning
> 3. Creating and thinking critically
>
> *Areas of learning*
>
> 1. Communication and language
> 2. Personal, social and emotional development
> 3. Physical development
> 4. Literacy
> 5. Mathematics
> 6. Understanding the world
> 7. Expressive arts and design
>
> Source: DfE (2023b).

The quality of early education can have a positive impact on children's future outcomes throughout their education and beyond. According to Mathers et al. (2016), disadvantaged children who attend good early childhood education can catch up with their peers, and since many children in care come from disadvantaged households, this is also true for them. To support CLA, early childhood practitioners, such as the child's key person and/or the designated person from children's social care, should contribute to any assessment of the child in accordance with the Early Help Assessment or local authority assessment framework, and attend multi-agency and strategy meetings about the child's learning and development. Together with the child's social worker and caregivers, practitioners will develop a Personal Education Plan (PEP) for children aged 3–5. Early Years Pupil Premium (EYPP) funding is available for disadvantaged children, including CLA, in order to support their educational needs. However, it is significantly lower than the equivalent for school-aged children. The purpose of this government funding will be discussed later in this chapter.

> *Reflective Questions*
>
> 1. How important it is that CLA have access to good quality early childhood provision?
> 2. Why do you think this?

The National Curriculum

The National Curriculum for England is the statutory set of subjects, standards and attainment levels for primary and secondary schools. It is organised into Key Stages and at the end of each stage children are formally assessed on their academic performance (Table 7.3).

A statutory guidance for local authorities, entitled Promoting the Education of Looked-After Children and Previously Looked-After Children (DfE 2018), provides guidelines for supporting the educational achievement of CLA or care experienced children. It outlines the duties that local authorities, Virtual School Heads, directors of children's services, and social workers must perform to comply with the law. Furthermore, Keeping Children Safe in Education (DfE 2024a) provides statutory guidance for schools and colleges regarding their responsibilities for safeguarding and promoting the welfare of children under 18 years of age. Additionally, it includes statutory requirements relating to safer recruitment practices. Everyone has a duty to safeguard children, and the emphasis is placed on this responsibility. It is the priority of everyone who works in schools and colleges to ensure that their practice is child-centred and that they understand their role in this.

> *Reflective Questions*
>
> 1. What measures can be taken to ensure the curriculum is inclusive and equitable for CLA?
> 2. How can teacher training be improved to better support CLA?

Schools, settings, and other organisations are regulated to ensure that all children receive high-quality education and care. The Office of Standards in Education, Children's Services and Skills (Ofsted) inspects services that provide education and skills for all learners and

Table 7.3 Key Stages in relation to age and school years

Key Stage	Age (approximately)	School years
Key Stage 1	5 to 7	1 and 2
Key Stage 2	7 to 11	3 to 6
Key Stage 3	11 to 14	7 to 9
Key Stage 4	14 to 16	10 and 11

Source: DfE (2014).

regulates services that care for children and young people (Ofsted 2024). Ofsted also publishes their inspection reports and they are accessible to all, to help raise the overall quality of education, training, and children's care. In the 2022-2027 strategy, Ofsted has a set of priorities to work towards to help improve lives by raising standards in education and children's social care. They aim to have inspections that raise standards, permit right-touch regulation, share insights through research, present evidence-based early years education, keep children safe, keep up to date with sector changes, ensure openness and accessibility and maintain a skilled Ofsted workforce. This is relevant for CLA because the quality of provision in education and children's social care determines the level and standard of care, support and nurturing CLA receive and this also shines a spotlight on what does not work well and highlights what settings and organisations need to do to improve their practice. Ofsted has recently come under criticism following the death of Ruth Perry, the headteacher of a primary school. A review conducted by the Education Committee (UK Parliament 2024) states that Ofsted and the government must rebuild trust and make significant changes in the way school inspections are conducted.

Pupil Premium and Pupil Premium Plus

In Chapter 9, we will discuss further the Pupil Premium (PP) that is aimed at supporting children from disadvantaged backgrounds, including CLA, to reach their full potential in their educational outcomes. The education of children in care is funded through a Pupil Premium Plus (PPP) grant allocated to Virtual School Heads to support CLA's educational needs as outlined in their PEP.

The PP was first introduced in 2011 and was paid directly to all state-funded schools to support their intake of disadvantaged children and young people who were already eligible for free school meals and for children who had been looked after continuously for more than six months (Read, Parfitt and Macer 2022). These funds were intended to be used to improve the academic achievement and attainment of children from disadvantaged backgrounds, thereby reducing the poverty attainment gap (Gorard, Siddiqui and Huat See 2021). Schools are increasingly being judged on the educational results of children receiving PP. The Children's World Report (2020) states that governments have been attempting to improve the educational attainment of poorer children for decades and that several stakeholders are considering whether this type of funding should be discontinued.

CLA are also entitled to receive the PPP which is a central government grant paid annually by central government to the local authority responsible for the care of the child. This is then allocated to Virtual School Heads to spend on educational activities that support the diverse needs of CLA (DfE 2024b). A key point in this process is that the PPP grant is used for support and interventions which are based on needs identified in the child's PEP. The Virtual School Head is responsible for ensuring that the statutory document is reviewed at least twice per year by professionals. However, although the PPP is used in the way the Virtual School Heads deem to be the most appropriate for a CLA, the administration and internal procedures of varying local authorities can unintentionally create inconsistencies,

Table 7.4 Funding allocated to schools and local authorities for the 2023-2024 financial year per child

Type of funding	Amount allocated per year
Early Years Pupil Premium (EYPP)	£353
Pupil Premium (PP)	£1455 for primary-aged children and £1035 for secondary-aged children
Pupil Premium Plus (PPP)	£2530

Source: DfE (2024b).

leading to the ineffectiveness of this funding (Read, Parfitt and Macer 2022). Navigating and coordinating the PEP process are demanding. The task of organising multi-agency meetings to discuss the needs of the child, the effective completion of the PEP form and ensuring that this funding is allocated in the most appropriate manner for the child all seem desirable when working in this multi-agency manner, however, it does present some challenges. The use of different technologies, systems, and forms across different local authorities makes this an extremely complex and challenging endeavour (NAVSH 2019). According to Evans et al. (2017), it is also challenging to demonstrate whether and to what extent educational outcomes have improved as a result of this funding and whether the interventions intended to support these outcomes need to be reviewed for effectiveness and rigour. Table 7.4 shows the amounts of funding allocated per child for the 2023-2024 financial year.

Children's Social Care Reforms

In March 2021, the government initiated an independent review of Children's Social Care, as outlined in its manifesto. As well as this report, the Child Protection in England and the Competitions and Markets Authority reports were also significant and were published in 2022. The Child Protection in England report offered recommendations from the national Child Safeguarding Practice Review Panel review into the deaths of two children: Star Hobson and Arthur Labinjo-Hughes. The Competition and Markets Authority was to address the concerns about the lack of suitable placements for CLA (Community Care Inform 2024).

In response to these three reports, the Department for Education published the Stable Homes, Built on Love strategy in 2023, which outlined the government's strategic plans to improve children's social care (DfE 2023a). With the additional investment of £200 million for the subsequent two years, the government proposed plans involving six ambitions of reform. Some £45 million of this additional investment is being used for a Families First Start Pathfinder programme in up to 12 local areas in England to develop a new Family Help service and make changes to front-line child protection practice. The six ambitions of reform are:

1. Family Help service provides the right support at the right time so that children can thrive with their families.
2. A decisive multi-agency child protection system.

3. Unlocking the potential of family networks.
4. Putting love, relationships, and stable homes at the heart of being a child in care.
5. A valued, supported and highly skilled social worker for every child in care.
6. A system that continuously learns and improves and makes better use of evidence and data.

A national framework for children's care, as well as a consultation on the social work workforce, was also released by the government. This Children's Social Care National Framework (DfE 2023d) has been designed to bring together in one document the overarching purpose of children's social care and what needs to be achieved to support the most vulnerable children in our society. This is statutory guidance for local authorities when delivering social care. This National Framework enables all professionals to have a shared understanding of what children's social care is and what it should look like. This National Framework outlines the purpose of children's social care:

> support children, young people and families, to protect children and young people by intervening decisively when they are at risk of harm and to provide care for those who need it so that they grow up and thrive with safety, stability and love.
> (DfE, 2023d, p. 12)

This National Framework not only brings together the purpose of social care, but also includes principles by which children and their families should be supported (DfE 2023d), showing the enablers that act as the foundation of good practice, and the outcomes that should be achieved. The principles to be followed are:

1. A child's welfare is the most important thing of all.
2. Children are asked about their wishes, and they are listened to and responded to.
3. Children's social care works with whole families.
4. Children are raised by their families, with the family networks or in family environments wherever possible.
5. Local councils work with other people to understand what children, young people and their families need.
6. Local councils are committed to acting fairly for everyone.

Aspects of the children's social care system that facilitate effective support and practice for children and their families are identified as enablers. The first enabler refers to multi-agency working and emphasises the importance of different agencies, such as local authorities, and others, such as the police, health services, and all aspects of education, including voluntary organisations, working together in an efficient and prioritised manner. Professionals across all agencies to be able to provide high-quality care and support must work together to raise aspirations, establish a shared approach to provide appropriate support, make sure children's voices are reflected in their practice, and determine the level of support, challenge, and accountability that will enable all agencies to work together effectively.

This National Framework is to be used in conjunction with the Working Together to Safeguard Children statutory guidance (DfE 2023e) which places statutory duties and responsibilities on agencies to safeguard and promote the welfare of children. The guidance provides details about what organisations and agencies must do to help, protect and promote the welfare of all children and young people in England. It focuses on multi-agency expectations for all professionals working with children and young people, parents and families to work towards a shared responsibility, learn with and from each other, provide appropriate services to help families, acknowledge and appreciate differences and challenge each other (Northumberland Children and Adults Safeguarding Partnership 2024). Additionally, this National Framework is also intended to be followed alongside the Special Educational Needs and Disability (SEND) Code of Practice: 0 to 25 years (DfE and DoH 2015), produced by the Department for Education and Department of Health. This places duties on local authorities to integrate education, training and health and social care to improve the quality of provision, in a joined-up approach, for children and young people with special education needs and disabilities. The principles from these statutory guidance documents reflect the expectations for practice as outlined in the National Framework.

Leadership in all aspects of the children's services sector is the second identified enabler. Leaders should empower and support the larger social care workforce to achieve the best possible outcomes for children and their families. Third, and finally, the children's social care workforce must be equipped and effective to achieve the best possible outcomes for children and their families (DfE 2023d).

This National Framework also identifies four outcomes relating to areas of a child's life where children's social services can provide the most effective support (DfE 2023d). As well, it reflects the belief that the best support a child can receive is from their family. There is a strong focus on the family to provide the best for their children, but it is not always possible for children to stay with their family and, when they cannot, they will be placed in loving, stable homes elsewhere.

THE NATIONAL FRAMEWORK'S FOUR OUTCOMES

Outcome One: Children, young people and families stay together and get the help they need

In addition to assisting families to stay together, children's social care provides parents with the support they need to care for their children safely. It is essential that practitioners listen to the children and their families to determine what kind of support is most appropriate for them. By doing so, practitioners are incorporating the views of parents into the child's safety plan. Additionally, this outcome emphasises the importance of respecting a family's culture and challenging all forms of discrimination. Furthermore, practitioners recognise the importance of education for children and the potential of education to help them achieve their full potential.

*Outcome Two: Children and young people are
supported by their family network*

Children's social care will support a child's family network when families are experiencing problems. In times of family difficulty, wider family members such as grandparents, aunts and uncles can often provide essential love, stability, and safety for children. Practitioners can support these wider family members to strengthen relationships or to repair ones in difficulty. For children, this means they will be asked who they consider their family and how their family network can care for them. Kinship care refers to the raising of children by a member of a family network.

*Outcome Three: Children and young people are
safe in and outside of their homes*

It is stated clearly in the National Framework that children's social care aims to keep children safe at home, where they live, in their wider community, and online. Children will be asked about their safety and well-being at all stages of their care experience, and practitioners will act swiftly to protect those at risk. For children to answer these questions honestly, practitioners must build positive, trusting, and strong relationships with them.

*Outcome Four: Children in care and care leavers have stable,
loving homes*

It is the responsibility of children's social care to provide them with a loving home if they are not able to live with their birth family or a family member. It is imperative that these homes offer love, care, protection, and stability. It is also important for children to receive support in understanding their feelings and dealing with trauma and adversity. Care leavers' ability to achieve positive outcomes and realise their potential is dependent upon the support they receive while in care.

Reflective Questions

1. What are your thoughts on the National Framework in improving the lives of CLA?
2. What are the potential economic and social impacts of the National Framework?
3. What is the potential long-term impact of this on CLA?
4. What are the challenges of implementing these reforms in practice?

Despite this, the National Society for the Prevention of Cruelty to Children (NSPCC 2024) reports that placement unsuitability and instability are still issues facing CLA. There are some CLA who remain in placements that do not meet their individual needs and there are many more who often move from one placement to another. As we have discussed in previous chapters, disruptions in placements can prevent children from forming attachments and positive relationships with adults, which can harm their overall emotional well-being (Rahilly and Hendry 2014). Additionally, the children's social care workforce is unstable, with record vacancies of 22 per cent (7,900 vacancies) and agency rates of 18 per cent (DfE 2023f; Murphy 2024). This instability within the workforce is concerning and the major changes identified in the government's reforms to children's social care are greatly needed. It should be noted, however, that the Munro Review of Child Protection identified similar changes more than a decade ago.

To help rebuild and restabilise the social work profession, the government must consider the public image of child protection social workers in England. According to Murphy (2024), the poor public image of the profession of social workers created by the media and political commentary was directly preventing potential candidates from seeking employment in the field of child protection. This not only reduces the number of professionals in the workforce but ultimately means that those existing professionals are being overstretched in their efforts to fill the employment gaps. This also increases the need for agency workers. Indeed, the Stable Homes, Built on Love strategy expresses the need to better inform people about how social workers work within their sector, to help raise public awareness. However, it does not provide enough information about how this will be accomplished and what exactly will be achieved. Murphy (2024), in research examining this government reform from the perspectives of social workers, found that 45 per cent of the participants estimated that they spent less than 10 per cent of their workweek visiting or working directly with children and that the remaining time was spent "writing about it".

Support for Care Leavers

In England, a care leaver is a young person aged 18 years who is no longer required to live in foster care and is entitled to ongoing support from the children's services after they leave care. According to Capstone Foster Care (2024), there are approximately 10,000 care leavers each year in the United Kingdom. However, the government has faced criticism about the way that care leavers are supported. The campaign, "End the Care Cliff" is supported by many famous celebrities who want the government to provide further support for care leavers and to be more aware of the difficulties experienced by these young people when leaving the care system. Become (2024), the national charity for CLA and care leavers, is lobbying the government to rethink the notion that at 18 years old all support is removed, and care leavers face the "care cliff" which can in itself be a very traumatic time due to the upheaval. Support, advice and guidance for CLA before they reach leaving age, as we have discussed in previous chapters, includes social, emotional and behavioural aspects of development. As a result of the literature and research embedded in various policies, we are aware of the importance of this to overall healthy development. Nevertheless, there is a need for more governmental transitional support to assist care leavers in adjusting to life outside of care and becoming independent.

Care leavers aged 18 who wish to pursue further education will be eligible to receive a living allowance from their local authority. As stated in the government's press release, "Long-term Strategy Launched to Fix Children's Social Care" (DfE and the Rt Hon Claire Coutinho 2023), the leaving care allowance has increased from £2,000 to £3,000, an above-inflation increase to help them set up home independently. Young people aged 19 years will be eligible for a bursary through the 16-19 Bursary Fund scheme. This has replaced the Education Maintenance Allowance. Additionally, there may be other avenues of support from their college, depending on the local education authority (Care Leavers Association 2024).

Additionally, there is an apprenticeship bursary that is intended to remove any financial barriers for care leavers in accessing and completing apprenticeships. The bursary is paid by the Education and Skills Funding Agency to the apprenticeship training provider, who then passes it on to the apprentice within 30 days. Apprentices should be given the opportunity to inform training providers about their care leaver status; however, if they do not wish to disclose their status to their employer, the payment to the employer will not be made (DfE 2023g).

> *Reflective Questions*
>
> 1. Do care leavers need more support when accessing further or higher education?
> 2. What other alternatives could the government consider in improving the educational outcomes of care leavers?

Summary

Professionals must be knowledgeable about government legislation, policy, and guidance to properly support the children they work with by providing high-quality education, care, and practices that comply with the law. Children from our most vulnerable group in society are protected by these statutory requirements. As a crucial aspect of child-centred practice, multi-agency collaboration is essential, with professionals from a variety of disciplines working collaboratively towards a shared goal in order to ensure the best outcomes for CLA. A teacher is not a social worker, and a social worker is not an educational psychologist. Since each discipline is highly trained and competent in its field, knowledge and understanding need to be shared to support CLA in reaching their full potential.

Different types of government funding are available for children from disadvantaged backgrounds to help them meet their educational goals. These funds can be used by schools, settings, and organisations to provide the added layer of support that can help narrow the poverty achievement gap. However, this approach will only be effective if the funds are allocated effectively and used to pay for resources, approaches, and interventions that are designed specifically to meet the needs of the children it is intended to support. Professionals from all disciplines must be able to address the challenges they face in being able to meet the needs of CLA, and the government must understand their frustrations. In our role as professionals, we must also be aware of the importance of supporting care leavers and that the government should provide, along with financial aid to these young people, more transitional support when starting to live independently.

References

Become. (2024). National Care Leavers Week. Available at: https://becomecharity.org.uk/become-the-movement/our-campaigns/national-care-leavers-week/

Capstone Foster Care. (2024). Care Leavers: Investing in the Long-Term Care of Children through the Capstone Care Leavers Trust. Available at: https://www.capstonefostercare.co.uk/news-and-blogs/investing-in-the-long-term-care-of-children-through-capstone-care-leavers-trust

Care Leavers Association. (2024). Support while Accessing Further and Higher Education. Available at: https://www.careleavers.com/what-we-do/young-peoples-project/acessingeducation-2/#:~:text=If%20you%20are%20a%20care%20leaver%20and%20entering,agreed.%20This%20does%20not%20have%20to%20be%20repaid

Children's World Report. (2020). Children's Views on their Lives, and Wellbeing in 35 Countries: A Report on the Children's Worlds Survey, 2016-19. Available at: https://isciweb.org/wp-content/uploads/2020/08/Childrens-Worlds-Comparative-Report-2020.pdf

Community Care Inform. (2024). Children's Social Care Reforms. Available at: https://www.ccinform.co.uk/practice-guidance/childrens-social-care-reforms/

DfE (Department for Education). (2014). National Curriculum. Available at: https://www.gov.uk/government/collections/national-curriculum

DfE (Department for Education). (2018) Promoting the Education of Looked-After and Previously Looked-After Children. Available at: https://www.gov.uk/government/publications/promoting-the-education-of-looked-after-children

DfE (Department for Education). (2023a). Children's Social Care: Stable Homes, Built on Love. Government Consultation Response. Available at: https://www.gov.uk

DfE (Department for Education). (2023b). Early Years Foundation Stage. Available at: https://www.gov.uk/early-years-foundation-stage

DfE (Department for Education). (2023c). Development Matters: Non-statutory Guidance for the Early Years Foundation Stage. Available at: https://www.gov.uk/government/publications/development-matters--2

DfE (Department for Education). (2023d). Children's Social Care National Framework. Statutory Guidance on the Purpose, Principles for Practice and Expected Outcomes of Children's Social Care. Available at: https://assets.publishing.service.gov.uk/media/657c538495bf650010719097/Children_s_Social_Care_National_Framework__December_2023.pdf

DfE (Department for Education). (2023e). Working Together to Safeguard Children 2023: Statutory Guidance. Available at: https://www.gov.uk/government/publications/working-together-to-safeguard-children--2

DfE (Department for Education). (2023f). Children's Social Work Workforce, 1st October 2022 to 30th September 2022. Available at: https://explore-education-statistics.service.gov.uk/find-statistics/children-s-social-work-workforce/2022

DfE (Department for Education). (2023g). Apprenticeships Care Leavers' Bursary Guidance. Available at: https://www.gov.uk/government/publications/apprenticeships-bursary-for-care-leavers/apprenticeships-care-leavers-bursary-policy-summary

DfE (Department for Education). (2024a). Keeping Children Safe in Education: Statutory Guidance for Schools and Colleges on Safeguarding Children And Safer Recruitment. Available at: https://www.gov.uk/government/publications/keeping-children-safe-in-education--2

DfE (Department for Education). (2024b). Guidance – Pupil Premium: Overview. Available at: https://www.gov.uk/government/publications/pupil-premium/pupil-premium#:~:text=Pupils%20in%20state%2Dfunded%20schools%20in%20England%20attract%20the%20service,2024%20to%202025%20financial%20year

DfE and DoH (Department for Education and Department of Health) (2015). Special Educational Needs and Disability (SEND) Code of Practice: 0 to 25 years. Available at: https://www.gov.uk/government/publications/send-code-of-practice-0-to-25

DfE and the Rt Hon Claire Coutinho. (2023). Long-Term Strategy Launched to Fix Children's Social Care. Available at: https://www.gov.uk/government/news/long-term-strategy-launched-to-fix-childrens-social-care#:~:text=In%20addition%20to%20the%20recruitment,find%20and%20maintain%20loving%20relationships

Early Years Coalition. (2023). Birth to 5 Matters. Available at: https://birthto5matters.org.uk

Evans, R., Brown, R., Rees, G., and Smith, P. (2017). Systematic Review of Educational Interventions for Looked-After Children and Young People: Recommendations for Intervention Development and Evaluation. *British Educational Research Journal*, 43(1), 68-94. DOI: 10.1002/berj.3252

Gorard, S., Siddiqui, N., and Huat See, B. (2021). Assessing the Impact of Pupil Premium Funding on Primary School Segregation and Attainment. *Research Papers in Education*, 37(6), 992-1019. DOI: 10.1080/02671522.2021.1907775

Mathers, S., Hardy, G., Clancy, C., Dixon, J., and Harding, C. (2016). *Starting Out Right: Early Education and Looked After Children*. London: University of Oxford/Family and Childcare Trust,

Murphy, C. (2024). The Dangers of Reactionary Attitudes Emanating from High Profile Child Welfare Cases. *Child Protection and Practice*. Available at: https://doi.org/10.1016/j.chipro.2024.100013

NAVSH. (2019). *The Virtual School Handbook*. Available at: https://navsh.org.uk.

Northumberland Children and Adults Safeguarding Partnership. (2024). Summary of changes: Working Together to Safeguard Children 2023. Available at: https://proceduresonline.com/trixcms1

NSPCC (National Society for the Prevention of Cruelty to Children). (2024). Impact of Being a Child in Care. Available at: https://learning.nspcc.org.uk/children-and-families-at-risk/looked-after-children

Ofsted (2024). About Us. Available at: https://www.gov.uk/government/organisations/ofsted/about#:~:text=Ofsted%20is%20the%20Office%20for,for%20children%20and%20young%20people.

Rahilly, T. and Hendry, E. (eds) (2014). Promoting the Wellbeing of Children in Care: Messages from Research. National Society for the Prevention of Cruelty to Children. Available at: https://clok.uclan.ac.uk/14634/1/promoting-wellbeing-children-in-care-messages-from-research.pdf

Read, S., Parfitt, A., and Macer, M. (2022). Breaks in the Chain: Using Theories of Social Practice to Interrogate Professionals' Experiences of Administering Pupil Premium Plus to Support Looked After Children. *Oxford Review of Education*, 49(5), 604-619. DOI: 10.1080/03054985.2022.2124963

UK Parliament. (2024). Ofsted and Government Must Rebuild Trust and Make Major Changes to School Inspections, Education Committee Says. Available at: https://committees.parliament.uk/committee/203/education-committee/news/199622/ofsted-and-government-must-rebuild-trust-and-make-major-changes-to-school-inspections-education-committee-says/#:~:text=Ofsted%20'marking%20its%20own%20homework,base%20it%20collects%20during%20inspection

8
Everyday superheroes

CHAPTER AIMS

This chapter will explore the role of everyday superheroes in the lives of Children Looked After (CLA) and how different professionals are perceived by CLA. By the end of this chapter, you will be able to do the following:

- Identify the characteristics of everyday superheroes.
- Understand the roles of different professionals who support CLA.
- Explore the perceptions CLA may have of different professions and adults.

Keywords

perceptions, professional and personal characteristics, superheroes, views

Introduction

In this chapter, we will explore the power of superheroes and what it means to be a superhero to a Child Looked After (CLA). In our opinion, all people have the power to be superheroes and make the lives better for children. However, some people may be harder to convince of their power than others. In the official definition, a superhero is defined as "someone who has done something very brave to help someone else" (*Cambridge English Dictionary* 2024), which we feel is quite fitting for the opening of this chapter in exploring the different superheroes out there helping CLA. Yet, as you will discover in this chapter, who qualifies as superheroes for adults and professionals may not be the same as the superheroes for CLA, given their experiences and circumstances. In this chapter, we aim to share the perspectives of CLA and understand why they hold certain impressions of the professionals and practitioners who are there to help them. This chapter will follow the story of Kaitlyn to help understand the perspectives of CLA.

Characteristics of a Superhero

We start this chapter by explaining some of the characteristics of superheroes shared with us by children aged between 4 and 13 years old. All of these children are children who have experienced little to no adversity and remain in the care of their families. The children were asked what makes a superhero a superhero and Figure 8.1 shows their responses.

What is refreshing to see is that children who have not experienced adversity like CLA have a very imaginative view of superheroes, they perceive them to be similar to those they find on television or in films and comic books, the typical depiction of people in suits, flying around and saving the world from mass destruction by evil villains. However, when CLA are asked to describe the characteristics of a superhero, there were obvious differences to what had been previously shared (Figure 8.2).

For CLA, the image of a superhero has some of the characteristics identified by the non-CLA, However, there is a greater focus on the person having contact with the superhero. The characteristics shift from what the superhero looks like with the superpowers to more how the superhero makes people feel and the actions they do for other people. What is interesting is that the CLA place a focus on being happy and protected, which is something other children did not really pay much attention to. The CLA identify that superheroes are "not evil or bad", they keep "the nasty people away" and "make all the scary people disappear and keep you safe". These characteristics are reflective of the CLA's background and experiences, the longing to feel safe and protected and away from nasty, bad, scary people who want to harm them.

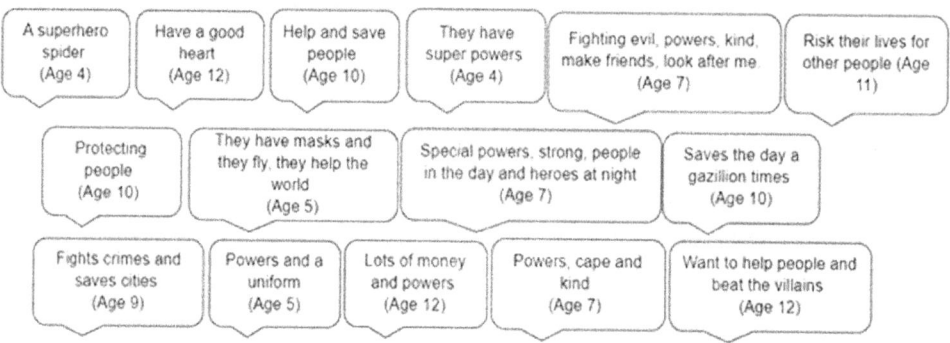

Figure 8.1 Children's responses to the question, "What makes a superhero?"

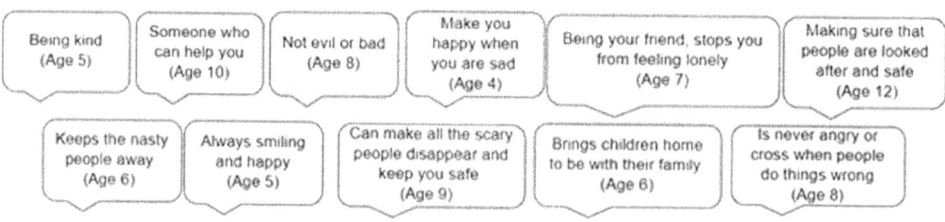

Figure 8.2 CLA's responses to the question, "What makes a superhero?"

Reflective Questions

1. With this in mind, if children were to name a person or group of people who fit their characteristics of a superhero, who would that be?
2. Why do you believe that these people are seen to be superheroes to the child?

The Perspectives of CLA

When exploring this concept with CLA and other children of similar ages, it is clear that there are differences of opinion, but this is also the case between adults and professionals who are involved with children. We use the term "everyday superheroes" to identify the "people who do something very brave to help someone else". In society, there are typical roles associated with this definition which are likely to be professionals you thought of when reflecting on the questions above. Figure 8.3 shows some, not all, that will commonly and widely be agreed on.

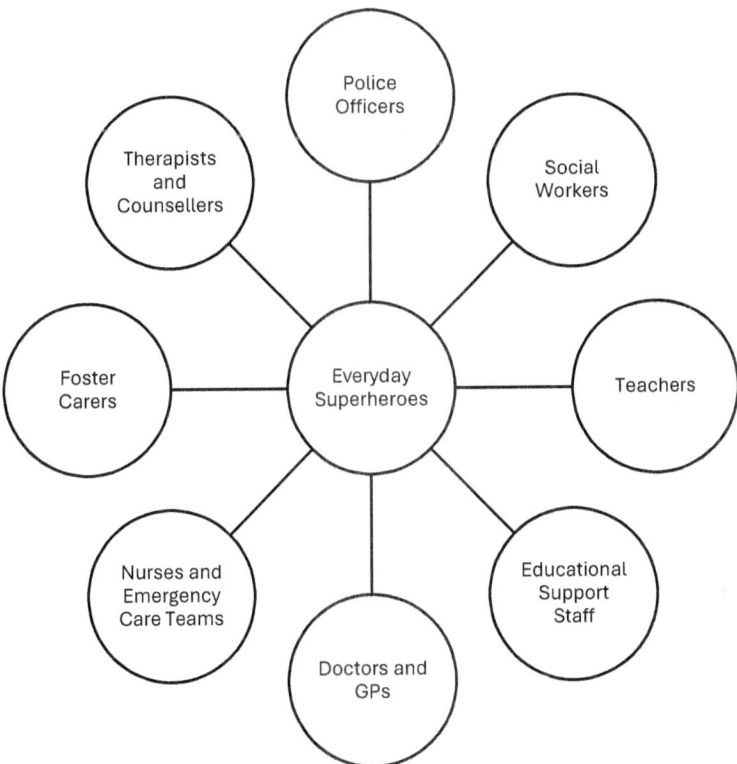

Figure 8.3 Examples of everyday superheroes

When we think of CLA and the people in place to help and support them, to be their advocates and to "save the day", these are the professionals and people who generally come to mind. However, we need to think about CLA and their experiences with these professionals and, as a child, would they really categorise these professional roles and actions as those of a superhero?

Case studies 10.1–10.3 will tell Kaitlyn's story.

> **CASE STUDY 10.1**
>
> Kaitlyn was 3½ years old when the police broke down her front door, arrested her parents and removed her and her two siblings from the family home. Kaitlyn witnessed her parents being dragged from their home, her mum had been holding her sister when the police came, and a police officer took her crying from their mum and kept Kaitlyn from following her parents. Kaitlyn and her siblings were in a police station for several hours while they waited for a social worker to take them to an emergency foster care placement.

Reflective Questions

In this scenario...

1. *Would Kaitlyn believe that the police were trying to help them?*
2. *Would she feel that they have come to save the day?*
3. *What impact could this situation have on a child's perception of police officers in the future?*

It is not uncommon for children to become fearful and mistrusting of the professionals that everyone else would expect to feel safe around. Although there are no official statistics, The Safeguarding Hub (2022) reports that each year hundreds of children in the United Kingdom are removed from their family homes by police officers following an incident report being filed. For CLA, and in the case of Kaitlyn, there may, until the point of removal, have been little or no involvement with police or social workers by the family. Like most, even CLA may have an image of police being there to help and save people, but for a child who has witnessed the police or social workers removing them from their family and the people they love, this will have a lasting traumatic effect on them. This will often leave CLA feeling resentful, untrusting, and even scared of the professional services that are in place to protect them. For CLA, it is not uncommon for their superheroes to be those that professionals deem inappropriate. Figure 8.4 identifies some superheroes from the perspective of CLA.

Now we know this, let us look at Kaitlyn's story a little more.

Parents
- For CLA, thier parents are the ones who have been a consistent person for them.
- Despite professionals deeming them inappropriate, for CLA they will have some form of attachment and loyalty to their parents.
- The behaviour they have witnessed from the parents may be all they know and accept this as normal behaviour from adults.

Neighbours and other members of the community
- Often there are other adults in the community or neighbourhood who recognise that a child is at need or at risk.
- Whilst some people will report signs and suspicions, without evidence, people in the community are less likely to report their suspicions to the authorities.
- Instead we see neighbours and other members of the community performing acts of kindness to children, such as giving them food and treats, bringing over hand me down clothes, offering to baby sit.
- These acts will responate with children and allow them experiecne kindness and relief from problems they may be facing at home.

Charities and volunteers
- Now we would expect different charities and volunteers in the community to have training and recogonition of safeguarding, especially being able to spot signs and symptoms of abuse. However, this is not as easy as you may think. Parents and children can become experts in masking and hiding these signs and symptoms.
- For a family who are struggling to feed their children, they may access food banks and places where meals are provided for free.
- In these cases, CLA will view these people as a life line, they are the ones who are making sure that they are eating and having meals. Regular volunteers may build positive relationships with the children helping to biuild bonds of trust.

Figure 8.4 Some examples of everyday superheroes for CLA

CASE STUDY 10.2

Kaitlyn and her two siblings were allocated a social worker (Jay) who met them at the police station. Several police officers had been taking turns to sit with the children and bring them toys. Kaitlyn regularly asked for her parents and wanted to see them. Her younger siblings aged 2 and 8 months, were upset at first but soon played with the toys. After a period of time, Jay took Kaitlyn and her siblings to Donna and Jason's house. Jay explained that Donna and Jason would be looking after them while she and the police decided what to do next. Kaitlyn had never met Donna and Jason before; they had a house and not a flat like her home.

Here we see some of the experiences and emotions Kaitlyn felt when being at the police station, not knowing what is happening to her and her parents, but also the confusion at why her siblings seem unaffected by the situation. These feelings of confusion are common for many children in this situation. As rational adults and professionals working with children, we know that removal from the family home is the worst-case scenario and only done if necessary, but this is not so simple to explain to a 3½-year-old child who has been traumatically taken from her parents. As identified in previous chapters, children will only be removed if absolutely necessary (Children Act 1989) which leads us to our next reflective questions:

> *Reflective Questions*
>
> 1. What could the police officers taking turns to look after the children do to help Kaitlyn feel less confused?
> 2. How could Jay help Kaitlyn through this traumatic and stressful period?
> 3. How could Kaitlyn feel more prepared for being moved to foster care?

Almost all children and young people who are placed in care in the United Kingdom are cared for by foster caregivers, most of whom are not biologically related to them. Of the 83,840 children living away from the family home on 31 March 2023, 57,020 of those CLA were recorded as living with registered foster families (DfE 2023). What this translates to is 57,020 children being placed with families that are unknown to them, they are complete strangers when first meeting them. Until this point of first entering foster care, the child will have developed difficulty in their relationships with adults, as can be seen from the case study so far. According to Kaip, Ireland and Harvey (2022), foster carer relationships can be challenging for CLA, especially as it can be considered normal practice for children to experience multiple foster placement moves Therefore, developing trust and an understanding of the child and their circumstances is often the hardest task for foster carers, as without this they will struggle to develop a positive relationship with the child. So where do we go next? What can professionals and other significant adults do to help this?

> *Reflective Questions*
>
> *Think back to other chapters in this book:*
>
> 1. Which ones have helped you to develop an understanding of the needs of CLA when building trusting relationships?
> 2. What strategies could the foster carers apply to help Kaitlyn and her siblings settle in and feel as though they belong?
> 3. What can social workers and other professionals do to help promote positivity through these transitions?

CASE STUDY 10.3

Donna and Jason were experienced foster carers, they had cared for many children in their home. They had lots of toys and games for the children to play with. Donna asked Kaitlyn what her favourite toys were. Kaitlyn said dolls, and said at home she used to play with her dolls for hours at a time, feeding them, brushing their hair, and changing their clothes. Donna asked Jay if she could bring some of these from Kaitlyn's home, however, Jay informed her that the house was inaccessible due to the nature of the police investigation. Donna tried to identify a doll that was similar to Kaitlyn's doll from home to hold and play with.

> *Reflective Questions*
>
> 1. Why do you think Donna did this?
> 2. What impact do you think this had on Kaitlyn?

It can be understood that small acts of kindness go a long way with children to build their trust and confidence in the adults around them. As identified in Chapter 4, children need consistency and trust in their caregivers to be able to develop positive attachments with them. Although a simple act of finding a similar toy or having their own toy may seem insignificant in comparison to their experiences, consistent small acts of understanding will help the CLA to feel seen and valued by the people caring for them (Hughes 2018). Over time, factors such as carer patience, attempts to spend enjoyable quality time together and getting to know each other can help facilitate positive outcomes for the CLA (Kaip, Ireland and Harvey 2022).

In Chapter 9, we will review the roles and responsibilities of significant professionals in the lives of CLA, for example, teachers and designated teachers, and Virtual School Heads. We have also reviewed family structures and in particular the roles of families (Chapter 6) but here seems a good time to review the roles and responsibilities of other professionals that CLA will have contact with.

Roles and Responsibilities of Professionals involved with CLA

Police

The police have a duty of care to protect the public from harm and criminality, in particular children. As detailed in the HMIC (2016) report, "In Harm's Way: The Role of the Police in Keeping Children Safe", it is the responsibility of the police force to work with other agencies to safeguard children, investigate crimes that have been committed against children and ensure that protective action is taken where necessary. But what does this actually mean? And what can we expect police officers to do to protect children?

According to the Children Act 1989, police have a duty of care to make enquiries into circumstances where they suspect child abuse and neglect have occurred or are occurring. They are duty-bound to refer all suspicions and reported cases to the local authority to promote engagement and support from social services. Where abuse and neglect can be evidenced, it is the responsibility of the police to prosecute offenders and bring them to justice for the crimes they have committed against children.

Social Services

According to the Departments for Education and Health (DfE and DoH 2015), social workers and social services as a whole are responsible for being the intermediatory link between multiple agencies working together for the best interests of children. Where children are at risk of harm or abuse, it is the job of social workers to assess the level of risk that the child faces and, where possible, support the families by directing them to other professionals and support strategies to help the children remain with the family. Social workers may be allocated to families on a temporary basis following a referral from other professionals, meaning that once the family have actioned the causes for concern, they are discharged from social worker intervention. Where children are deemed at a higher risk of harm or abuse, a social worker will be allocated to the child and the family on a longer-term basis to provide more consistent support. Should the family not be able to make the necessary changes, social services will make the application for the child to be removed from the family home and placed in the care of the local authority. This process is reviewed in more detail in Chapter 1.

When a child is placed in the care of the local authority, it is the role of the social worker to find the child a suitable place to live with people who can meet the needs of the child. As reviewed in both Chapters 1 and 6, there are several different options when placing children to live, but it is the job of social services to assess all the possibilities available for care for the child and choose the best environment for the child. While in the care of the local authority, the child's social worker is their advocate, ensuring the best decisions are being made for the child in all aspects of their lives, including education, medical needs, and treatment, contact and communication between birth family and siblings.

From this we can identify that the key roles for local authority social workers and social services is to provide a care plan, review health and arrange placements for children. Breaking this down we can see a clear set of responsibilities for social workers for each role.

Care Planning

This involves facilitating open and honest communication between CLA, their families, carers and other professionals to collectively plan and review the care that the child is receiving while in the care of the local authority. Critical decisions need to be made and where all parties cannot agree, the social worker will have the overriding decision. The purpose of care planning is to do the following:

- ensure that children and their families are treated with openness, honesty, and understanding about the decisions made for them;
- provide clarity in the allocation of tasks involving the child, ensuring that everyone knows who is responsible for which aspects and who is authorised to decide on behalf of the child. The child's parents and carers must be consulted in this decision-making process, as it allows a more harmonised approach to children's care.
- demonstrate accountability in line with the Children Act 1989, ensuring all the functions of the local authority are exercised.
- create a care plan for each child which has considered their individual needs and wishes but also details all of the above points for everyone to review.

Health

Social workers are required to ensure that CLA's good health is maintained, and arrangements are made to monitor children's health throughout their time in care. A health plan should be created to assess the child's health and level of health intervention and should include:

- an assessment of the child's physical, emotional and mental health;
- a detailed history of the child's health and any contributing factors from their background that could be important to children's future health promotion;
- existing plans in place for the child's medical needs, including dental and therapeutic approaches.

It is important that these plans are reviewed by the social workers and others identified every six months for children under the age of 5 and every 12months for children over the age of 5.

Placement

As we have discussed, at several points throughout this book so far, children being placed outside of the family home by social services occurs only in extreme cases where it is not in the child's best interest to remain within the family. When placement is agreed upon, it is the role of the social worker to ensure where possible:

- the placement allows the child to live near their home;
- the placement does not disrupt their education, therefore not requiring them to change schools;
- they remain living with their siblings (see more about this in Chapter 6);
- the placement provides accommodation, which is suitable to the needs, and for children who are disabled, ensuring there are accessible facilities;
- the child remains living within the local authority (Coram 2023).

In doing this, children can maintain a sense of community and belonging as well as maintain connections with their family and community relationships.

Health Professionals

For each CLA, there should be a named health professional who is responsible for liaising with different health professionals, depending on the needs of the child (DfE and DoH, 2015). They will coordinate the health care professionals to complete the required health assessments and reviews for CLA as well as ensure the timeliness of the health assessments are completed and to a high-quality standard. They will also act as a conduit for the child's carers to access health services if they are finding it difficult to do so, overall, the designated health professional will act as an advocate for the CLA's health needs and

112 Advocating for Children Looked After

Figure 8.5 Health professionals involved with CLA

requirements. CLA will access different health professionals who will support not only their physical health but also their emotional and mental health, meaning that the child may potentially have contact with a number of health services (Figure 8.5), which is why the designated health professional is important to effectively coordinate these.

Not all CLA will access all of these services, however, while in care the children will undergo regular reviews which contribute to the care and health plans produced by the child's social worker. As previously mentioned, this is every six months for a child under 5 years old and every 12 months for children aged 5 and over.

> *Reflective Questions*
>
> 1. How important are police, social workers and health professionals for the overall care and development of CLA?
> 2. Do these identified professionals play a more important role than the child's family or foster family?
> 3. What challenges may you come across when working with these professionals to support CLA?

Challenges for Professionals Working with CLA

There are a number of identified challenges for multi-agency working with the best interests of CLA in mind. The most common is communication and everyone being aware of the role they play and how they feed their information and support back to everyone else. Information between all professionals and carers should be shared openly and honestly between all parties to ensure that robust plans and support can be put into action. Poor communication can lead to information being missed and this means lost opportunities to meet the individual needs of the CLA.

However, what can be deemed as a more significant challenge to professionals working with CLA is the reputation that professionals have, derived from their line of work. As we discussed earlier in this chapter, it is extremely difficult for CLA and parents to trust and build relationships with professionals, such as social workers and police, as they can be seen as the professionals responsible for breaking up and separating families. Even health professionals who have reported concerns, from the perception of children and families, could be considered to be people not to trust to look after the child's best interests. For CLA, professionals can be seen as the "nasty people", the "bad people", the "scary people" identified earlier in the chapter. To overcome this perception, it is important for professionals, especially social workers, to maintain a kind and consistent approach. The child may never fully understand the judgements made by social workers and police, but it is their responsibility to show honesty and kindness to CLA and, in time, the child may develop a strong and attached relationship with their social worker.

Summary

We can see from this chapter that perception is a powerful tool. It has the ability to transform how we see professional roles and the importance they play in the lives of CLA. It is important as we continue our work and support of CLA that although we view professionals as everyday superheroes, these perceptions might not be shared by CLA and their families. With this in mind, professionals need to consider their influence on CLA and how their involvement in their lives can transform how the child will see the world and engage with the professionals in it. The biggest takeaway from this chapter is that every person who has contact with CLA has the power to be an everyday superhero. Everyone, from neighbours next door to designated professionals, has the possibility of influencing the lives of CLA but we all have a responsibility to ensure that the influence we have is through positivity and in the best interests of the child. In doing this, we hope with time that CLA and their families will see the importance of these roles and come to see these people as superheroes for themselves.

References

Cambridge English Dictionary. (2024). Available at: https://dictionary.cambridge.org/dictionary/english/superhero

Children Act 1989. c.31 and 44. Available at: https://www.legislation.gov.uk/ukpga/1989/41/contents

Coram. (2023). Local Authorities' Duties in Relation to Looked After Children. Available at: https://childlawadvice.org.uk/information-pages/local-authority-duties-to-looked-after-children/

DfE (Department for Education). (2023). Children Looked After in England Including Adoption: 2022 to 2023. Available at: https://www.gov.uk/government/statistics/children-looked-after-in-england-including-adoption-2022-to-2023.

DfE and DoH (Department for Education and Department for Health). (2015). Promoting the Health and Welfare of Looked-After Children. Available at: https://assets.publishing.service.gov.uk/media/5a7e01c4e5274a2e8ab453b5/Promoting_the_health_of_looked-after_children_statutory_guidance_consult....pdf

Hiller, R.M., Halligan, S.L., and Meiser-Stedman, R. (2020). Supporting the Emotional Needs of Young People in Care: A Qualitative Study Of Foster Carer Perspectives. *British Medical Journal*, 10(17). DOI: 10.1136/bmjopon-2019-033317

HMIC. (2016). In Harm's Way: The Role of the Police in Keeping Children Safe. Available at: https://assets-hmicfrs.justiceinspectorates.gov.uk/uploads/in-harms-way.pdf

Hughes, A. (2018). *Building the Bonds of Attachment*. 3rd edn. Lanham, MD: Rowman & Littlefield.

Kaip, D., Ireland, L., and Harvey, J. (2022). "I Don't Think a Lot of People Respect Us" – Police and Social Worker Experiences of Interagency Working with Looked-After Children. *Journal of Social Work Practice*, 37(1), 29-44. https://doi.org/10.1080/02650533.2022.2036109

Safeguarding Hub (2022). Police Protection: A Practical Guide. Available at: https://safeguardinghub.co.uk/police-protection-a-practical-guide/

9
Teacher or Facilitator

CHAPTER AIMS

In this chapter, we will explore the role of practitioners supporting Children Looked After (CLA) in schools and educational settings. By the end of this chapter, you will be able to do the following:

- Understand different strategies for supporting CLA in schools and settings.
- Explore the role of teachers and practitioners in meeting the needs of these children.
- Identify key educational requirements for supporting CLA.

Keywords

ACE-aware, designated teacher education, facilitator, learning and development, practitioner, teacher, trauma-informed, Virtual School Heads, Virtual Schools

Introduction

All children have the right to equality of opportunity in their education (UN 1989). The United Nations Convention on the Rights of the Child (UNCRC) came into force in the United Kingdom in 1992 and has 54 articles that encapsulate civil, political, economic, social and cultural rights. In particular, Article 28 states that every child has the right to an education. Yet, Children Looked After (CLA), because of a myriad of factors, face multiple barriers to learning, some of which we have discussed in previous chapters. Children who are looked after or are care experienced are at a higher risk of having poorer education outcomes. Therefore, we must understand the different strategies for supporting children who are looked after in schools and other settings.

Outside of the family environment, children spend most of their time at school or early childhood settings. Therefore, the teacher and practitioner roles are fundamental for children's development and for children looked after, the relationship with their teacher is even more important. We will explore a few strategies and approaches that schools have adopted

116 Advocating for Children Looked After

to meet the needs of CLA in a way that is more holistic and inclusive, which include trauma-informed and attachment-informed schools. Virtual Schools and Virtual School Heads have an essential role in supporting the education of children who are in care and in this chapter we will examine their effectiveness along with their limitations. Table 9.1 offers definitions of the roles of the various educational professionals and practitioners we will be discussing.

Strategies and Approaches

In order to assist children and young people who have experienced early adversity and who are looked after, Brighter Futures (2024) aims to provide all school professionals with the training they need to provide support to these children and young people. This training has been designed to be flexible and can be delivered in multiple contexts, all of which are designed to help build a welcoming, respectful and fair environment in schools by addressing the key topics in Figure 9.1.

It is important to have a deeper awareness of what each of these key topics involves. The child protection systems section delves into the different policies and organisations and explores how they are grounded in promoting children's rights as identified in the UN

Table 9.1 Definitions of roles of education professional

Term	Definition
Teacher	A person who helps others acquire knowledge, competencies or values
Facilitator	A person who supports and guides learners, teachers and other stakeholders in various educational settings
Designated teacher	A teacher in the school setting who is responsible for promoting the educational achievement of CLA
Virtual School Head	A person in charge of promoting the educational achievement of CLA in the local authority

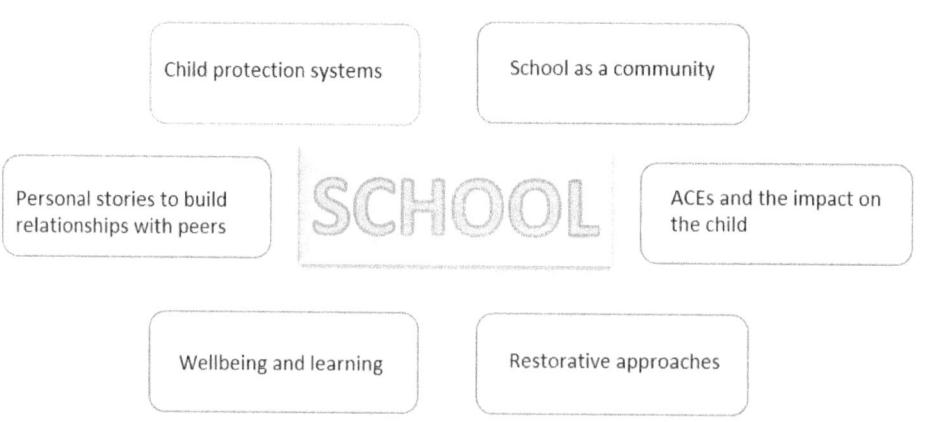

Figure 9.1 Key topics of the Brighter Futures (2024) training and support

Convention of the Rights of the Child (UNCRC 1989). It explores the concepts of citizenship, inclusion, and the ways in which families, caregivers, and the broader community can work together to achieve a shared vision. For schools and settings to achieve educational equity, there needs to be a whole-school approach to well-being that emphasises the importance of intersectionality. As a part of the section on ACEs, the concept of ACEs from a psycho-social perspective is explored to show professionals what the impact of early adversity are and how they can work to address them.

A significant number of children who are looked after have a history of adversity, which may impact their achievement when they find themselves in an educational setting. Therefore, professionals need to be aware of the relationship between well-being and learning when dealing with these children. If a child is suffering from poor levels of well-being and is struggling to function in the school environment, there is a good chance they are not going to be able to reach their full potential without additional support. The school's approach to behaviour needs to come from a rational place and be inclusive to support positive outcomes for children who have been placed in care. It is important to recognise that a one-size-fits-all behavioural approach is not conducive in this sense and that everyone working in education needs to acknowledge the different behaviours and the challenges that CLA can create. A school's behaviour policy should reflect an understanding of the impact of ACEs as well as an acknowledgement of the role that teachers and schools can play in supporting children who have been looked after. It is more important to consider this than the level of educational attainment and how good the school looks in the league tables. In addition, the personal stories of children at school section focuses on the idea that children have the potential to learn from one another and to recognise and value the different perspectives that each will have, based on their respective backgrounds and experiences, as well as the importance of children being able to learn from their peers. This is one of the most important aspects of building a sense of community as it allows the children to start to feel like they are part of a group and that they belong.

Attachment-Aware Schools

Increasingly, there are a number of schools that are using the fundamentals of attachment theory in order to meet the needs of CLA, as well as other vulnerable children, in their classrooms. For teachers to be able to work more effectively with their children with challenging behaviour, they need to have a deeper understanding of attachment theory and its implications in practice. In line with the National Institute for Health and Excellence Care's recommendation (NICE 2015), all schools and childcare providers should be appropriately trained to ensure that they can meet the needs of children and help them to form meaningful attachments.

As a result of this recommendation, guidance for training teachers requires all trainees to be taught the importance of emotional development and attachment issues as part of the training process (DfE 2016). In 2024, the Initial Teacher Training Core Content Framework replaced this, which defines the minimum entitlement of all trainee teachers. There are five core areas: behaviour management, pedagogy, curriculum, assessment, and professional behaviours, which are aligned with the eight Teachers' Standards (DfE 2024). In relation to supporting the emotional development and attachment issues with all children, particularly for children from disadvantaged backgrounds in Standard 1 Setting high expectations, trainee teachers will learn they can impact and improve children's well-being, motivation and behaviour. In Standard 7 Manage behaviour effectively, trainee teachers will learn how to develop positive and safe environments for children and to build trusting relationships.

The Attachment Aware Schools project was intended to be a collaborative intervention between academics and school-based practitioners with the overall aim of promoting practitioner awareness of attachment theory and the impact it has on child behaviour and learning (Rose et al. 2019). The Attachment Aware Schools programme in the East Midlands was designed by the Virtual School to provide support to a range of other schools and settings in the area, with the overall goal of developing innovative approaches to pedagogy to improve the outcomes of CLA in education. There is no doubt that a clear understanding of attachment theory, along with the ways in which this knowledge can be applied to current pedagogy or practice, will not only be beneficial for children in need but will also benefit all children, since it provides the underpinning for creating a nurturing and safe environment where children can thrive

Kelly, Watt and Giddens (2020), in their evaluation of this Attachment Aware Schools programme, reported on the greatest impacts stemming from implementing this approach schools. It has been noted that the first impact has been the re-evaluation of schools' current policies and systems, as well as the inclusion of more robust pastoral policies that have proved to be successful. In addition to this, several schools reported that the attempt to develop a more nurturing and safer environment in their schools has resulted in physical changes to the school, with many classrooms now having safe areas for students to spend time in during the school day. This has reshaped our perceptions of space and how we as educators use classrooms, and offers the opportunity to look through the child's lens on how they perceive their space is invaluable. In addition, it was noted that this approach allowed schools to focus on identifying key adults, and in some settings, the Designated Teacher role had been redesigned to better meet the needs of the children and young people. The teachers also reported that they saw an improvement in the children's behaviour and that they found that the children are learning to manage their behaviour more effectively and are able to self-regulate more often after the intervention was implemented. There is no doubt that CLA are happier and more confident in school when they have positive and nurturing relationships with their teachers, along with feeling safer in that environment, which is evident in better behaviour and improved learning outcomes. The final impact to note is that the awareness of the importance of building positive attachments and relationships with CLA in their classrooms and the integration of this into their practice has opened up opportunities for extending relationships with parents and carers as well. There was a growing realisation among teachers that bridging the gap between school and home was of paramount importance. Teachers were able to remove previous negativity and communicate more transparently and inclusively with parents and carers as a result of these extended relationships, which led to increased trust and stronger relationships between teachers and parents.

Although this programme has been successful, it has also had its limitations. Practitioners and educational settings may become overwhelmed by the number of policies, strategies, and initiatives, resulting in changes that are "incomplete and uncoordinated" (Banerjee, Weare and Farr 2014, p. 718). While the achievement rate continues to improve year after year, it is important for the schools and settings involved to change how they teach and become more nurturing, to increase the achievement rate. As a result, all aspects of the school's ethos, pedagogy, and practices have been reshaped to reflect the attachment narrative, embracing, in essence, the idea that children will learn, develop, and flourish in an enabling environment.

Emotion Coaching

As part of the Attachment Aware Schools framework, Emotion Coaching has been promoted as a tool to provide specialised targeted support to children. It was first identified by Gottman, Katz and Hooven (1996) as a technical and philosophical approach to emotions as part of their work on a natural parenting strategy. In their analysis, they found that children who were assisted by their parents in understanding their emotions were able to self-regulate and were more motivated and attentive. Based on these observations, Gottman et al. identified different styles of approaches based on varying levels of empathy and guidance (Figure 9.2).

Figure 9.2 Styles of responding to emotions

Source: adapted from Romney, Somerville and Baines (2022).

Through a further study of parents, Gottman et al. (1996, cited in Romney, Somerville and Baines 2022) were able to identify five steps:

1. Becoming aware of the child's emotion.
2. Recognising emotional moments.
3. Listen empathetically and validate the child's feelings.
4. Help find the words the child needs to label the emotion.
5. Set limits while exploring strategies.

Several of these steps have been slightly adapted and developed into a school-friendly programme that is used in some schools in the United Kingdom to support children and young people in developing emotional resistance, empathy, and problem-solving skills. As a result of research into the effectiveness of Emotion Coaching in schools, many teachers and practitioners feel that this is an appropriate and useful intervention (Krawczyk 2017; Rose, McGuire,-Snieckus and Gilbert 2015).

> Reflective Questions
>
> 1. How might your understanding of attachment theory impact your practice?
> 2. Why is it important to bridge the gap between school and home through transparent communication?

Trauma-Informed schools

A trauma-informed approach is becoming more prominent in policy to minimise the negative impacts of traumatic experiences and improve mental and physical health outcomes (Office for Health Improvement and Disparities 2022). Trauma-informed schools support children and young people with trauma or mental health challenges. It is understood by these schools that troubled behaviour has the potential to act as a barrier to learning in the classroom. To create a mentally healthy, safe and welcoming environment for the children, they foster a climate of communication, build positive relationships, and minimise unnecessary reminders of trauma. Felitti et al. (1998) state:

> Rising numbers of children are presenting with mental health difficulties in schools and current teaching environments are struggling to keep up. Many children have a high ACE score (meaning multiple adverse childhood experiences) known to leave children at risk of mental and physical ill-health later in life and even early death.

With the help of appropriate training, schools can become trauma-informed and, as a result, will be able to understand and mitigate the damaging effects that traumatic experiences have on CLA. This involves the whole school, not just the class teacher, and all those who work or volunteer within a trauma-informed school share the overall ethos and understanding of recognising and supporting the behaviour and emotional well-being of CLA.

> Reflective Questions
>
> 1. What strategies do you think trauma-informed schools use to create mentally healthy environments for CLA?
> 2. Why is it important for the entire school community, not just the teacher, to be involved in trauma-informed practices?
> 3. Which stakeholders within and surrounding schools should be included when working on the well-being of CLA?
> 4. What do you think the reasons for schools not following this approach are?

Based on the review of the existing literature, Smith, Cameron and Reimer (2017) evaluated the effectiveness of ACEs and trauma-informed approaches to education, as well as how ACEs can impact educational outcomes. Based on academic research within the fields of health and social care, as well as children's services, it was concluded that there tended to be a low percentage of reports about causality between the interventions used to support children and young people with adverse childhood experiences and the positive outcomes they achieved. There could be a variety of reasons why this may be the case, including the number of variables involved in considering a particular child, their ACEs, and their academic success rate. These approaches are not without criticism. Smith, Cameron and Reimer (2017) argue that simplistic assumptions about attachment are a point of critique in social work theory. In many cases, these assumptions can lead to an over-reliance on narrow interpretations of attachment theory, without taking into account the broader and more complex realities of human relationships and development.

For each of these strategies and approaches, there is a similar pattern or tone that has emerged that is common to all of them. An important aspect of this ideology is the idea that a child should be supported by the community rather than just by a single individual. An exosystemic perspective sees children's development as taking place within an ecological system that promotes their agency, learning, and interaction through everyday proximal events and our understanding of the influence of social environments on their development (Rose et al. 2019).

Theraplay Project

According to the Theraplay Institute (2024), Theraplay is an approach that uses the natural patterns of play interactions between an adult and child to help build relationships, self-esteem, and trust. The aim of this approach is to support the development of a child's behavioural, social and emotional skills. This intervention lends itself well to the work of educational psychologists and is therefore endorsed by the Association for Play Therapy.

The interactional focus of this approach is on four essential qualities in adult-child relationships: structure, engagement, nurture and challenge. Structure provides boundaries for the child, engagement builds a shared enjoyment and connection with another adult, nurture provides a secure base for the child to build upon, and challenge allows the child to take appropriate risks in order to develop mastery and confidence. This attachment-based approach was analysed to determine whether it was effective in helping CLA in terms of their social and emotional well-being. Francis, Bennion and Humrich (2017) concluded that the key mechanism is the psychological skills necessary to deliver this therapeutic intervention. Children's social and emotional skills can be developed through the support of schools, settings, and psychology services available to them. In turn, this affected the way in which they engaged with their education.

Nurture as a Strategy

According to Bradbury and Grimmer (2024), the approaches we use in schools and settings determine what we ultimately want for all of our children and society. In previous chapters, we have discussed the role of attachment theory in explaining children's need for love and care. In addition, we discussed the need for professionals to build positive and responsive relationships with the children with whom they work. The concept of nurture must now be explored, especially in the early years of a child's life. As discussed in Chapter 4, professionals need to be aware of the developing brain. It is essential for all professionals to maintain a focus on the CLA's learning and development when caring for very young babies and children. We are not unfamiliar with the concept of nurture, and research on nurturing emotional relationships has been largely influenced by early childhood pioneers such as Bowlby (1988) and Ainsworth (1978). In recent years, the field of early childhood has grown steadily, as academics and researchers have begun to explore many different aspects that encompass the crucial period of childhood and have built upon previous research. For instance, Conkbayir (2023) and Grimmer (2023) explore emotional attachment through neurobiology and how nurturing, responsive, empathic relationships create long-lasting and positive impacts on a child's development.

The development of children's emotional well-being is deeply rooted in their brain architecture, and supporting children to form loving attachments promotes a sense of self, a love of learning, social skills, a sense of self-confidence, as well as empathy and emotional understanding (Bradbury and Grimmer 2024). This has links to the concept of emotional intelligence which was introduced by Goleman (1995) to describe how we manage our own and others' emotions to be socially successful. Through his work, teachers have been able to prevent, detect and redirect potentially destabilising emotions in children in a safe and nurturing manner. To promote emotional intelligence in children, we need to teach them self-awareness, self-regulation of emotions and empathy skills. Early intervention is fundamental to improving the outcomes of CLA. When working with babies and younger children, professionals need to consider the unique socialisation needs of these children because they need the essential social skills and attitudes to live within a community (Minett 2017).

CASE STUDY 9.1

Ollie, who is 7 years old, recently started attending Hope Hill Primary School. Having moved from one foster family to another one, he could no longer travel to his original school due to the distance. This is his second school this year. He misses his other foster family and his own bedroom. As a result of his uncertainty about the length of time he would be staying in this new family, he found it difficult to fall asleep at night. It was while Ollie was in class that his teacher asked him to join a small group of children for a reading activity, but he refused to participate. It was comfortable for him to sit where he was. Ollie was embarrassed when other children started sniggering. Suddenly, he jumped up, kicked the chair backwards, and started to storm out of the classroom. A teacher told him to wait outside the headteacher's office and that his behaviour would not be tolerated. As a result of this outburst, he would also lose his "golden time" on Friday afternoon.

Reflective Questions

1. What could the teacher have done before meeting Ollie for the first time?
2. In your opinion, is this school behaviour policy inclusive?
3. Which strategy or approach could this teacher and the school implement to help support children with adversities?

Virtual Schools

The concept of Virtual Schools was first introduced in England in 2007 with the aim of supporting the education of children who are in care. A Virtual School is not a physical setting, but it is made up of a group of mainly teachers in a local authority who work in partnership with schools and other services in order to improve the educational outcomes for CLA (Sebba and Berridge 2019). It is important to note that CLA will still attend school as normal, however, they will be able to have this additional layer of support from the Virtual School. All local authorities in England were required to appoint a Virtual School Head since the Children and Families Act 2014 amended the Children Act 1989. These Virtual School Heads (VSH) are vital in ensuring that CLA have the opportunity to reach their full educational potential (DfE 2021). This role also involves being a source of advice and information for parents of CLA. As a result of non-statutory guidance, this has been further expanded through the inclusion of specific oversight of all CLA with an assigned social worker (DfE 2021). Children who are in kinship care, also known as family and friend care, are now included under this non-statutory remit, as of September 2024. As the name suggests, this is a situation where a family member or a friend looks after a child who is unable to be looked after by their birth parents.

An important function of the VSH is to identify all CLA by the local authority and know where they are educated and cared for (NAVSH 2019). Following the Revised Guidance for Virtual School Heads and Designated Teachers (DfE 2018, cited in Sebba and Berridge 2019), the responsibilities of VSHs are:

- Creating a culture of high educational aspirations;
- ensuring children in care access high quality education placement options;
- ensuring children in care have effective Personal Education Plans;
- monitoring the attendance and progress of children in care;
- ensuring that a "Children in Care Council", i.e., young people in care representing the interests of those in care, report on their educational experiences.

All local authorities are required to provide the resources, time, training and support needed for VSH to effectively perform their roles and to achieve the goals Virtual Schools have set out to achieve. As another layer of aid for the VSH, each school must also identify a designated teacher who will support individual children looked after in their schools to promote their education. In this way the child will have access to support within their school and also have the added aid provided by Virtual Schools (NAVSH 2024). This designated teacher will provide regular contact with the VSH and act as a point of contact for the Virtual School. The designated teacher will also provide support to CLA in their schools, helping them to access the full range of educational opportunities.

The charity, National Associate of Virtual School Heads works to improve educational outcomes for CLA through the sharing of research results and to promote the care and education of children currently in care and care leavers through training. NAVSH (2024) estimates that there are 150 Virtual Schools in England, each with its cohort numbers, and organisational and financial arrangements. There are many variables that affect the number of staff employed and the roles they hold, such as the number of young people in care and the context of the local authority. NAVSH represents them on a national level and has a common purpose in their work.

How Effective Are Virtual Schools?

VSH, as noted by Drew and Banerjee (2019) provide enhanced learning opportunities through one-to-one tutorials, mentoring, and extra-curricular activities. Additionally, one of the primary roles that was deemed to be pivotal in supporting CLA was that of raising awareness through the provision of continuous professional development training for both educators and social workers. This is an interesting issue and for many of us, it is fairly common sense that if we offer specific and bespoke training to raise awareness and understanding of, for instance, the effects of early trauma and neglect, it will enable teachers to approach behaviour management differently.

The education of children in care is funded through a Pupil Premium Plus (PPP) grant allocated to VSH to support the child's educational needs as outlined in their Personal Educational Plan. It is essential that all CLA have a Personal Educational Plan (PEP) as part of their care plan, which also includes the contact information for the child's VSH. Ofsted, the education inspection agency, then monitors and inspects these grants to ensure they are used in accordance with the child's Personal Educational Plan. While Ofsted's (2012) review of Virtual Schools found evidence of effective support for individual children and elements of enhanced stability and well-being, these elements varied from child to child. The review also acknowledged the financial constraints that ultimately resulted in limited resources impairing their provision, as well as the difficulty in defining the actual roles and responsibilities of Virtual Schools. However, despite the fact that Virtual Schools have been supporting CLA since the pilot programme was launched in 2007, there has been very little research conducted on the effectiveness of this role and its impact on children's educational outcomes.

Reflective Questions

1. What do CLA need from teachers and practitioners?
2. Do these children need education or nurture? Can they have both?
3. What role does a teacher play in a child's life?
4. Are teachers and practitioners able to meet the needs of these children?

To ensure the successful educational outcomes of CLA teachers, facilitators, designated teachers and VSH are all essential. Together, these roles have the potential to positively influence the lives and life trajectories of the children with whom they work. When defining a teacher, we can mostly agree that it is a person who helps others acquire knowledge, competencies or values. However, a facilitator supports and guides learners, teachers and other stakeholders in various educational settings. The traditional role of a teacher must merge with the role of the facilitator because they support not only their children, but also other teachers and professionals in various educational settings. As we have discussed in this chapter, some of the current strategies and approaches reflect this new role. It is not without limitations, however.

In a survey of teachers in England, Become (2018) found that 87 per cent (of 447 respondents) claimed that they did not receive any training about supporting CLA before they qualified as teachers; 31% felt they did not get enough support from children's services and 87 per cent reported that they had heard at least one colleague express negative generalisations about CLA in their classrooms. These statistics reflect how we as a society view CLA or care experienced children and how teacher training programmes are not properly equipping new teachers with the tools needed to best support these children in their classrooms. How can we expect teachers at the forefront of children's lives to respond to, and manage the many challenges these children face as well as be able to create an environment where they can learn, develop and thrive?

The aim of behaviour support strategies in schools and settings should be to encourage and reward the achievement of all children, and every school should have high expectations for every child, as well as knowledge of the best provision in order to meet their specific needs. These should be inclusive and serve as a framework for identifying when a child requires additional support to reach their goals. As an educator, it can seem as though schools are unfairly required not only to teach children academic skills but also to provide support and nurture so that they are emotionally healthy and able to learn. Even though it may seem to be a massive undertaking, if schools and settings cooperate with social care, health services, and other supportive external agencies, as shown in some of the examples provided in this chapter, CLA as well as other vulnerable children will not fall through the cracks. It is only through the collaboration of services that this can be prevented in order to improve outcomes for children.

Summary

Schools that provide a welcoming and safe environment and ensure effective collaboration between themselves and the children's sector improve the social inclusion and educational outcomes of CLA. However, it is important to note that this is not always the case for every school. In some instances, schools can have a negative and detrimental impact on children and their educational success. It is clear that the quality of the school environment is paramount. A whole school approach where children are supported in their socio-emotional development and where schools and settings have the opportunity to undertake effective training will benefit all children, not just CLA. As professionals, we need to understand that a child's attachment is not fixed. With the right support and consistency, children can develop the ability to change their attachments throughout their lives. Successfully establishing and sustaining attachments to the other key people influential in a child's life will ensure they reach their full potential. Some or all of these attachments may change as a child grows and develops as an emotionally healthy individual.

A better understanding of what impact ACEs may have on children's behaviour, social and emotional development, and physical and mental health can help people working with children in an educational context to address the challenges appropriately and lead to more positive educational outcomes, regardless of whether or not individual children can be identified as 'having' ACEs. As a result of changes in pedagogy, teachers and practitioners are practising more reflection and embracing a more holistic approach to working with children and young people.

References

Ainsworth, M.D.S. (1978). The Bowlby Ainsworth Attachment Theory. *Behavioural and Brain Science*, 1(3), 436-438.

Banerjee, R., Weare, K., and Farr, W. (2014). Working with Social and Emotional Aspects of Learning (SEAL), Associations with School Ethos, Pupil Social Experiences Attendance and Attainment. *British Educational Research Journal*, 40(4), 718-742. DOI: 10.1002/berj.3114

Become. (2018) Teachers Who Care (2018) Available at: https://becomecharity.org.uk/teachers-who-care-2018/

Bowlby, J. (1988). *A Secure Base: Clinical Applications of Attachment Theory*. London: Routledge.

Bradbury, A. and Grimmer, T. (2024). *Love and Nurture in the Early Years*. London: Learning Matters.

Brighter Futures (2024). Innovative Tools for Developing Full Potential After Early Adversity. Available at: https://webs.uab.cat/bf/the-project/

Conkbayir, M. (2023). *The Neuroscience of the Developing Child: Self-regulation for Wellbeing and a Sustainable Future.* Abingdon: Routledge.

DfE (Department for Education). (2016). A Framework of Core Content for Initial Teacher Training (ITT). Available at: https://www.gov.uk/government/publications/initial-teacher-training-itt-core-content-framework

DfE (Department for Education).(2018). The Revised Guidance for Virtual School Heads and Designated Teachers. Available at: https://assets.publishing.service.gov.uk/media/5a90354bed915d57d133580d/Revised_guidance_for_Virtual_School_Heads_and_designated_teachers__1_.pdf

DfE (Department for Education). (2021). Guidance: Virtual School Head Role Extension to Children with a Social Worker. Available at: https://www.fenews.co.uk/resources/guidance-virtual-school-head-role-extension-to-children-with-a-social-worker/ance: Virtual school head role extension to children with a social worker

DfE (Department for Education). (2024a). Children Looked After in England Including Adoptions – Reporting Year 2023. Available at: https://explore-education-statistics.service.gov.uk/find-statistics/children-looked-after-in-england-including-adoptions

DfE (Department for Education). (2024b). Initial Teacher Training (ITT): Core Content Framework. Available at: https://www.gov.uk/government/publications/initial-teacher-training-itt-core-content-framework

Drew, H. and Banerjee, R. (2019). Supporting the Education and Well-Being of Children Who Are Looked-After: What Is the Role of the Virtual School? *European Journal of Psychology of Education*, 34 (1), 101–121. https://www.jstor.org/stable/48698007

Felitti, V.J., Anda, R.F., Nordenberg, D., Williamson, D.F., Spitz, A.M., Edwards, V., Koss, M.P., and Marks, J.S. (1998). Relationship of Childhood Abuse and Household Dysfunction to Many of the Leading Causes of Death in Adults. The Adverse Childhood Experiences (ACE) Study. *American Journal of Preventative Medicine*, 14(4), 245-258. DOI: 10.1016/s0749-3797(98)00017-8. PMID: 9635069

Francis, Y., Bennion, K., and Humrich, S. (2017). Evaluating the Outcomes of a School-Based Theraplay Project for Looked After Children. *Educational Psychology in Practice*, 33(3), 308-322. DOI: 10.1080/02667363.2017.1234405

Goleman, D. (1995). *Emotional Intelligence.* New York: Bantam Books.

Gottman, J.M., Katz, L.F., and Hooven, C. (1996). Parental Meta-Emotion Philosophy and the Emotional Life of Families: Theoretical Models and Preliminary Data. *Journal of Family Psychology*, 10(3), 243-268. Available at: https://www.proquest.com/docview/614338785?accountid=14693&pq-origsite=primo&sourcetype=Scholarly%20Journals

Grimmer, T. (2023). Is There a Place for Love in an Early Childhood Setting? *Early Years*, 42(5), 1-14. DOI: 10.1080/09575146.2023.2182739

Kelly, P., Watt, L., and Giddens, S. (2020). An Attachment Aware Schools Programme: A Safe Space, and Nurturing Learning Community. *Pastoral Care in Education*, 38(4), 335-354. DOI: 10.1080/02643944.2020.1751685

Krawczyk, K.M. (2017). A Whole School Single Case Study of Emotion Coaching (EC) Training and the Impact on School Staff. University of Birmingham. Available at: https://www.proquest.com/docview/2344540709?parentSessionId=7r%2FDz%2BO8ls9HtRODgwbX61Oy3IWEeYCnGwt7zdvDiGO%3D&sourcetype=Dissertations%20&%20Theses

McIver, L. and Bettencourt, M. (2023). Virtual Schools for Care-Experienced Learners in Scotland: Reflections on an Emerging Concept in a New Context. *British Educational Research Journal*. DOI: 10.1002/berj.3988

Minett, P. (2017). *Children Care and Development.* 7th edn. London: Hodder Education.

NAVSH (National Association of Virtual School Heads). (2019). *The Virtual School Handbook.* Available at: https://navsh.org.uk

NAVSH (National Association of Virtual School Heads). (2024). About Us. Available at: https://navsh.org.uk

NICE (National Institute for Health and Care Excellence) (2015). Children's Attachment: Attachment in Children and Young People Who Are Adopted from Care, in Care or at High Risk of Going into Care. NICE guideline. Available at: https://www.nice.org.uk/guidance/ng26

Office for Health Improvement and Disparities. (2022). Working Definition of Trauma-Informed Practice: Guidance. Available at: https://www.gov.uk.../working-definition-of-trauma-informed-practice

OFSTED. (2012) The Impact of Virtual Schools on the Educational Progress of Looked After Children. Available at: https://assets.publishing.service.gov.uk/media/5a7f2487e5274a2e8ab4a603/The_impact_of_virtual_schools_on_the_educational_progress_of_looked_after_children.pdf

Romney. A., Somerville, M.P., and Baines, E. (2022). The facilitators and Barriers to Implementing Emotion Coaching Following Whole-School Training in Mainstream Primary Schools. *Educational Psychology in Practice*, 38(4), 392-409. DOI:10.1080/02667363.2022.2125933

Rose, J., McGuire-Snieckus, R., and Gilbert, L. (2015). Emotion Coaching: A Strategy for Promoting Behavioural Self-Regulation in Children/Young People in Schools: A Pilot Study. *European Journal of Social and Behavioural Sciences*, 13(2). DOI: 10.15405/ejsbs.159.

Rose, J., McGuire-Sniekus, R., Gilbert, L., and McInnes, K. (2019). Attachment Aware Schools: The Impact of a Targeted and Collaborative Intervention. *Pastoral Care in Education*, 37(2), 162-184. DOI: 10.1080/02643944.2019.1625429

Sebba, J. and Berridge, D. (2019). The Role of the Virtual School in Supporting Improved Educational Outcomes for Children in Care. *Oxford Review of Education*, 45(5), 538-555. DOI: 10/1080/03054685.2018.1600489

Smith, M., Cameron, C., and Reimer, D. (2017). From Attachment to Recognition for Children in Care. *The British Journal of Social Work*, 47(6), 1606-1623. Available at: https://www.jstor.org/stable/26612871

Theraplay Institute. (2024). About Theraplay. Available at: https://www.theraplay.org.uk/about

UN (1989). UN Convention on the Rights of the Child. Available at: https://www.unicef.org.uk/what-we-do/un-convention-child-rights/

10
Change in vision

CHAPTER AIMS

In this chapter, we will explore what we want for our children and what children want from us, the professionals and the government. By the end of this chapter, you will be able to do the following:

- Understand the importance of Continuing Professional Development and how to be a reflective professional.
- Explore the professional roles in supporting Children Looked After and families.
- Identify what improvements can be made in practice to better promote the voice and identity of CLA.

Keywords

child's voice, Continuing Professional Development (CPD), inequalities in education, reflective practice

Introduction

As the concluding chapter in this book, it seems fitting to explore what we want for our children and what our children want from us. We need to start with the question of what can, and should, we be doing in our practice as professionals to best support Children Looked After (CLA) in all aspects of their lives? In this chapter, we will offer recommendations on ways to raise awareness of CLA from research-based practice as well as from the child's perspective. Throughout this book, we have explored the need for professionals in all capacities to be highly trained in meeting the unique and often complex needs of CLA and shown how being a reflective professional is beneficial not only for professional standards but for the CLA we work alongside. There is a long road ahead in changing the narrative for CLA and the assumptions, stereotypes and prejudiced attitudes in our society, but we know it is a road that needs to be taken. We can start by reporting the positive aspects of CLA, celebrating their achievements rather than their failures, and enabling children to have their opinions and voices heard.

To effectively start our journey for improvement for CLA, we need to identify our own training needs, which are most commonly through Continuous Professional Development (CPD) across all children's professional services.

What Is CPD?

There needs to be a cohort of well-trained, and knowledgeable professionals within all areas of the children's workforce who can work effectively and collaboratively with other professionals, children and their families towards a shared goal. When we consider training for professionals, we need to consider the role of CPD. CPD is a process of gaining knowledge and skills beyond any initial training or qualification and then applying this new learning to practice to maintain or raise quality. CPD encompasses all learning activities, both informally and formally, that you may engage with to enhance your professional development. There is an intrinsic need for appropriate recognition of the overall value of effective CPD along with the multitude of benefits, not only for you regarding continuing your learning, training, and expertise but also for the CLA and the families you work alongside. The type of CPD required differs, as it is based on your own personal areas for development and training needs, which means that CPD requires a substantial amount of personal and honest reflection, therefore, reflection is a central feature of CPD (McArdle and Coutts 2010). There are many different examples of CPD, for instance, conferences, staff training sessions, observing others, online learning, books and journals, newsletters, classroom-based courses or workshops and professional discussions, to name a few.

> *Reflective Questions*
>
> 1. What CPD have you undertaken?
> 2. Did you benefit from this?
> 3. Did the CLA you work alongside benefit from this?

The Importance of Being a Reflective Professional

There are many definitions of reflection, mostly because reflection can take many forms. Moon (2004) defines reflection as providing opportunities for learning and an awareness of and clarifying thoughts in our personal and professional development. Sambell, Gibson and Miller (2010) suggest that reflection involves analysing and evaluating our experiences in order to find the lessons we need to learn. However, according to Bolton and Delderfield (2018), reflective practice is an ongoing attitude to life and work which allows individuals to learn from experience. Effective reflective practice will help you to feel good about what you do and how you do it by increasing the acceptance of and confidence in the changing landscape of your professional life.

There are many reasons why we engage in reflection, and these could include: doing things better next time, understanding what we are doing, acknowledging our training needs, seeing how we can do things differently and becoming self-aware. To be reflective means to engage in deep thought, often to construct a reflection of a situation or event. We can reflect on experiences from our practice, however, if we learn from our experiences and gain new knowledge of ourselves and our practice, we then become reflective professionals. Being a reflective professional means engaging with our reflections and learning from them, repositioning our assumptions, values and practice, and continually aspiring to think about ways to improve (Hanson 2012). This implies that being a reflective professional means having the skill to think critically as well as having acquired professional knowledge and attributes. According to PACEY (2024), a reflective practitioner does the following:

- celebrates their strengths and skills and acknowledges areas that need developing;
- takes professional responsibility for constantly improving the quality of their own practice;
- thinks about the way they work and why they choose certain ways of working;
- considers the impact of their practice on others;
- considers working in different ways and introduces new ways of working;
- plans how to maintain and develop their practice in future.

We should bear in mind, however, that in some areas of children's social care, professionals may find it difficult to incorporate all of the points above to become more reflective. As a result of the restrictions imposed on the workforce, this may seem to be a difficult task. Therefore, we must also take into consideration the leadership qualities that all professionals require in order to be able to change and improve their own practice and the practice of others. All of us are leaders in some aspects of our professions, and we must have the courage and determination to challenge areas of practice that do not support CLA effectively.

Developing our professionalism through reflective practice and ongoing CPD helps us all to expand our professional identity and, in a nutshell, our ability to reflect and evaluate practice. Reflective practice is a core concept for professionals supporting CLA, based on Schön's (1983) view of professionals 'reflecting in action' to think about their experiences and then 'reflecting on action' afterwards. The purpose of reflection is to assist professionals in understanding their work, shaping their practice, and learning from their experiences. A professional must have the confidence to reflect in action and consider what is actually happening and how it can be improved. Some less confident professionals may find it easier to reflect on action first. A study conducted by Ferguson (2018) on how professionals working with CLA reflect in action revealed that, at times, the demands of professionals' in-person work were so great that they could not even think about or reflect on their experience. The CLA they supported would not be their primary focus if they were to reflect in action. Ferguson found that professionals supporting CLAS had difficulty reflecting in action as they were so used to reflecting on action as a means of protecting themselves and making their work bearable. As a result, these professionals should be aware that this in itself is a limitation when reflecting on their practice. In light of the nature and demands of supporting CLA, it may not always be possible for them to reflect effectively in action.

Undertaking effective CPD can positively impact the lives of CLA as you are continually improving your practice by upskilling your professional portfolio, which, in turn, filters to the children you work with. Regular and effective CPD can enhance your confidence as a professional, which then increases your sense of professional identity. Your engagement with CPD will be able to demonstrate high levels of commitment as a professional which could be an important factor in promoting your career progression. All of this will drive your engagement with CPD but also inspire the people you work alongside to become effectively engaged. Ultimately, Bradbury (2022) states that the focus of your CPD should always be concerned with improving and supporting the outcomes for the children you work alongside.

Training and Development

It is the responsibility of the Virtual School Heads (VSH) to provide information, training, and guidance, not just for themselves, but also for all professionals who support CLA (DfE 2018, cited in Sebba and Berridge, 2019). During their study of professionals' experiences administering Pupil Premium Plus (PPP), Read, Parfitt, and Macer (2022) found that the extent to which the information, training, and guidance that were applied in practice was unclear. In their study, they found that professionals had access to a variety of types of information and training. As a result, it proved to be difficult for them to determine what would work best for them and the children they work with. Furthermore, some VSH and designated teachers in schools and settings had to spend time locating relevant and appropriate information and training, which meant they had less time to devote to the CLA they were supporting.

In previous chapters, we have discussed some types of training that can assist teachers and schools, including Emotion Coaching and Bright Futures. However, it is equally imperative that professionals undertake CPD in areas relevant to their practice in supporting CLA to achieve their full potential. As a means of supporting CLA, ACE awareness must be incorporated into all teaching qualifications. As part of their training, teachers should be aware of what being a CLA means to a child and his or her family. It is not just about meeting educational needs; it is also important to foster attachments that lead to a sense of security and safety for CLAs. For CLA to be able to learn in a classroom, teachers must first create an environment in which the children can learn.

Training for Teachers

We have already discussed in Chapter 5 that CLA thrive when they are cared for by adults who show a genuine interest in them and can form strong and positive relationships with them. We also reviewed the role of the teacher in supporting CLA in both Chapters 7 and 9, identifying how teachers need to be more aware of their role in supporting attachments in their education encounters with CLA. Currently, the Initial Teacher Training Core Content Framework requires that all trainee teachers be instructed on the importance of attachments. Despite this, we believe that a loving and nurturing approach to teaching should underpin our professional pedagogy and ethos to provide CLA with the highest possible opportunities for success.

> ### Reflective Questions
>
> 1. How could we be more loving and nurturing in our practice when supporting CLA?
> 2. How could our understanding of attachment change to better promote positive attachments and relationships for CLA?
> 3. What additional training do teachers need to be able to do this effectively?

Training for Early Childhood Practitioners

Grimmer (2021) emphasises the importance of a loving pedagogy in early childhood education settings and schools, as well as the importance of valuing and promoting children's best interests. Positive attachments form an important foundation for a child's development. If we understand the different ways in which children feel loved, the rights children have and the ways in which to empower children through love, we will be able to deliver a nurturing and loving pedagogy that places the child at the centre of our practice.

In Chapters 5, 7 and 9, we explored the Early Years Foundation Stage (EYFS) framework in great detail and identified what support is currently in place for CLA. However, we feel that more needs to be done for CLA than having a key person approach. A child-centred approach is needed, so instead of assigning a key person to each child, we should consider what each child wants and who they consider their safe person to be. As we talk about listening to a child's voice and recognising a child's expertise in their own lives, why not practise what we preach?

> ### Reflective Questions
>
> 1. How could we be more child-centred in our early childhood practice when supporting CLA?
> 2. How could our understanding of attachment change to better promote positive attachments and relationships for CLA?
> 3. What additional training do early childhood practitioners need to be able to do this effectively?

Training for Social Workers

In Chapter 8, we explored the roles and responsibilities of social workers and the impact their role has on CLA and their families. As the Children's Social Care Reforms (DfE 2023), discussed in Chapter 7, come into force, the hope is to bring in more professional social workers with widening skills and abilities to effectively support CLA. Social workers are currently trained to support not only the child but also the family. However, do social workers have the time and abilities to support families who are a low-level concern before it escalates to the child being removed from the family and entering the care system? To do this effectively, social workers must develop a deeper understanding of family backgrounds and differing circumstances as identified in Chapter 3, to be able to apply early intervention and support to families most in need and at risk.

> *Reflective Questions*
>
> 1. How could social workers be more aware of family's low-level needs?
> 2. How can social workers promote good relationships with families?
> 3. Are these requests on social workers realistic, given the demands of their profession?

So with these training requirements identified, we now need to further explore what CLA need us, as professionals, to do better to support them in their journeys through life.

What Do CLA Need Professionals to Do?

Change the Language

First, we need to consider the language we use with more care regarding the perceptions of the child. As discussed in Chapter 2, we should refer to CLA more inclusively and positively, we must change the landscape of the language we use because the language currently being used does not fit the nurturing narrative we claim to have. Changing language from being clinical in nature to becoming more nurturing will assist CLA in developing a positive sense of self, as well as reshaping social attitudes that are prejudicial and stereotypical.

Challenge Inequalities in Education

Second, there are inequalities in our education system that need to be addressed in order for the system to become inclusive and equitable for all children and young people and to reshape the pedagogy to be more inclusive of CLA's neurodiversity, as discussed in Chapter 4. Children's success in speaking and writing has come to define early performance in the primary school system. Regarding the Spelling, Punctuation and Grammar (SPaG) summative tests, according to Hammond (2019: 73), the "structural ideology of these tests has added to the marginalisation of children from socially disadvantaged backgrounds". Children who are least likely to be exposed to standard English in their daily lives and those who possess some elements of their own dialect are immediately placed at a disadvantage. The inability to meet the demands of these tests can negatively impact the well-being and sense of identity of children. There are also differences in attainment and achievement for children from disadvantaged backgrounds and, as we know, many CLA fall into this sector of the population and remain one of the lowest-performing groups in terms of educational outcomes (PALAC 2018). Most people are aware of this, especially those who are involved with CLA. There are always statistics and figures that completely support this. In comparison with their peers, care leavers may experience poorer employment and health outcomes after leaving school. Care leavers are also over-represented among the offender population and those who experience homelessness. Therefore, we need to focus on the positive achievements of CLA and care leavers so we can start to change educational assumptions and stereotypes.

Research is starting to demonstrate that there are many CLA who have positive experiences at school and are not part of that statistical data pool. Many CLA have positive experiences at school and are supported effectively to reach their full academic and social potential. These are schools that are inclusive and clear on the expectations and standards needed to continue to support CLA's well-being to improve their outcomes. A school might be the only stable and secure environment for CLAs, and professionals who are properly trained can provide CLAs with appropriate support and resources to ensure their success. In doing this, schools should maintain a deeper understanding of children's ACEs, trauma and neurodiversity.

Change the Structure of Educational Provisions

Following on from this, we need to consider replacing the alternative provisions in primary and secondary schools with specialist nurture programmes. Currently, CLA across primary and secondary schools are being removed from classes and learning due to their behaviour and inability to learn as a direct result of their ACEs. These children are at risk of leaving school with no qualifications and recognition of their abilities and achievements. We need to consider replacing these alternative provisions and children's removal from mainstream teaching with the nurturing and attachment-based practice we have advocated throughout this book. This is especially so for secondary school provisions as when children move from primary to secondary, the nurturing of children seems to diminish and be replaced with structure and sanctions.

Reform in Public Perception

In the media, over the years, there has been the occasional celebrity from the stage or screen who shares their personal stories about their experiences of being a CLA or care experienced. More recently, the British actor, Barry Keoghan has been hailed as aspirational by CLA. Through media interviews, this actor has been sharing his experiences from childhood to a career in film and television and this has started to dismantle the stigma attached to CLA. More former CLA need to share their stories to help reduce the negative perception of CLA. These children can start to understand that their identity and consequent labels in their lives do not define them or limit what they aspire to be when they are

Table 10.1 Biographies of high-profile former CLA cases

Name	Biography
Samantha Morton	The actress spent 10 years in foster care and credited Ken Loach's *Kes* for inspiring her acting career, showing that representation matters
Barry Keoghan	The actor spent seven years in the foster care system passing through 13 foster homes before entering the care of his maternal grandmother
Marilyn Monroe	Her mother, a single parent, was declared legally insane and Marilyn was sent to an orphanage for two years. She then lived with a family friend for four years.
Neil Morrisey	Neil and his brother had been removed from the family home, due to it being an unclean and neglected household and entered the care system
Eddie Murphy	Eddie and his brother were taken into the foster care system for around a year, due to his mother being ill in hospital
Steve Jobs	Steve grew up in the foster care system for a part of his life. Steve's biological parents were unmarried, and his mother gave birth to him in San Francisco. He was later adopted.

adapted from Children's Commissioner (2024).

older. When, as a society, we listen to these open, honest, and transparent narratives about life experiences from a range of diverse backgrounds, we can start to challenge our perceptions about stigma, identity, labels and language. The reasons for children being removed from their birth parents and entering care are varied but there is one common denominator – all children are blameless; it is not their fault, so why should they be forced to carry the stigma into adulthood? We need to promote more platforms for listening to people's stories to inform CLA and care leavers that they can go on to lead successful lives and be an inspiration for all subsequent CLAs. The circumstances of a child's birth or upbringing should not determine where and who children will become in adulthood.

Table 10.1 shows some high-profile CLA cases that can inspire others.

Actively Listening and Responding to CLA

Throughout the various pieces of legislation, policies and statutory guidance that govern our practice with CLA, it seems pertinent to discuss the role of the child's voice and how the voices of CLA are central to our work. A key component of this is recognising and valuing children's individual identities and acknowledging they may not yet know who they are or where they belong as discussed in Chapter 1 and Chapter 6. The Children's Social Care National Framework (DfE 2023), as discussed in Chapter 7, stipulates that one of the principles we need to follow is that children are asked about their wishes, and they are listened to and responded to. Additionally, CLA must feel empowered to complain about the service they receive and that these complaints are listened to and responded to. It was the Children Act 1989 that first introduced the rights of CLA in an attempt to reduce the abuse of children in children's social care settings. However, the number of complaints registered by CLA remains low, which could be due to a plethora of factors, including the imbalance of power CLA may experience. This means that the CLA's voice is not being allowed to be heard, nonetheless, there are still ways in which we can listen to children. Ofsted (2017, cited in Diaz et al. 2019) stated that almost one in ten CLA reported that their foster carers or professionals at children's homes rarely or never helped them when they were upset. Furthermore, Diaz et al. found that, even when CLA did complain or voice their opinions, this did not carry equal weight to the professionals and, consequently, they were not always listened to. This is of huge concern, and we need to examine how effective the guidelines and procedures are that are aimed at encouraging and supporting CLA to complain about the services they receive and discover what the barriers are. As discussed in Chapter 8, we call for all professionals supporting CLA to be held accountable for the overall welfare of CLA and to ensure that there is a level of transparency which enables children to be valued in our society.

Reflective Questions

1. Are professionals capable of actively listening and responding to CLA?
2. How can we challenge the perception in society of CLA with the resources we have?
3. How can schools and settings change their approach to nurturing CLA?
4. How will you change your language to positively promote your relationships with CLA?

Summary

We need professionals who consistently promote the value of education and provide emotional and social support to help CLA manage the complex demands of education and relationships and promote their own identity. CLA need to be provided with practical and financial support to help them do this. Obviously, this may be determined by the amount of funding that children's social care services and other agencies receive to effectively support CLA.

References

Bolton, G. and Delderfield, R. (2018). *Reflective Practice: Writing and Professional Development*. 5th edn. London: Sage.
Bradbury, A. (2022). What Is CPD? *Early Years Educator*. Available at: https://www.earlyyearseducator.co.uk/features/article/focus-what-is-cpd
Children Act 1989. c.31 and 44. Available at: https://www.legislation.gov.uk/ukpga/1989/41/contents
Children's Commissioner. (2024). A List of Incredible People Who Were Fostered, Adopted or in Children's Homes, Compiled by Lemn Sissay. Available at: https://www.childrenscommissioner.gov.uk/imo/your-stories/a-list-of-incredible-people-who-were-fostered-adopted-or-in-childrens-homes-compiled-by-lemn-sissay/
Dahlberg, G., Moss, P., and Pence, A. (1999). *Beyond Quality in Early Childhood Education: Postmodern Perspectives*. London: Falmer Press.
DfE (Department for Education). (2023). Children's Social Care National Framework: Statutory Guidance on the Purpose, Principles for Practice and Expected Outcomes of Children's Social

Care. Available at: https://assets.publishing.service.gov.uk/media/657c538495bf650010719097/Children_s_Social_Care_National_Framework__December_2023.pdf

Diaz, C., Pert, H., Alyward, T., Niell, D., and Hill, L. (2019). Barriers Children Face Complaining About Social Work Practice: A Study in One English Local Authority. *Children and Family Social Work*, 25(2). DOI: 10.1111/cfs.12702

Ferguson, H. (2018). How Social Workers Reflect in Action and When and Why They Don't: The Possibilities and Limits to Reflective Practice in Social Work. *Social Work Education*, 37(4), 415-427. DOI: 10.1080/02645479.2017.1413083

Grimmer, T. (2021). *Developing a Loving Pedagogy in the Early Years: How Love Fits with Professional Practice*. Abingdon: Routledge.

Hammond, S. (2019). *What Social Justice? Perspectives on Educational Practice Around the World*. London: Bloomsbury

Hanson, K. (2012). How Can I Support Early Childhood Studies Undergraduate Students to Develop Reflective Dispositions? Available at: https://ore.exeter.ac.uk/repository/handle/10036/3866 (accessed 20 November 2021).

McArdle, K. and Coutts, N. (2010). Taking Teachers' Continuous Professional Development (CPD) Beyond Reflection: Adding Shared Sense-Making and Collaborative Engagement for Professional Renewal. *Studies in Continuing Education*, 32, 201-215.

Moon, J. A. (2004). *Reflection in Learning and Professional Development: Theory and Practice*. Abingdon: RoutledgeFalmer.

PACEY (Professional Association for Childcare and Early Years). (2024). The Importance of Training and CPD. Available at: https://www.pacey.org.uk/training-and-qualifications/the-importance-of-training-and-cpd/

PALAC (Centre for Inclusive Education). (2018). Promoting the Achievement of Looked After Children and Young People in Lincolnshire. Available at: https://discovery.ucl.ac.uk/id/eprint/10094352/1/Carroll_palac-lincoln-case-study-2017-18.pdf

Read, S., Parfitt, A. and Macer, M. (2022). Breaks in the Chain: Using Theories of Social Practice to Interrogate Professionals' Experiences of Administering Pupil Premium Plus to Support Looked After Children. *Oxford Review of Education*, 49(5), 604-619. DOI: 10.1080/03054985.2022.2124963

Sambell, K., Gibson, M., and Miller, S. (2010). *Studying Childhood and Early Childhood*. London: Sage Publications.

Schön, D. (1983). *The Reflective Practitioner: How Professionals Think in Action*. New York: Basic Books.

Sebba, J. and Berridge, D. (2019). The Role of the Virtual School in Supporting Improved Educational Outcomes for Children in Care. *Oxford Review of Education*, 45(5), 538-555. DOI: 10/1080/03054685.2018.1600489

INDEX

A
abuse 3, 4, 29; *see also* adverse childhood experiences (ACEs)
academic functioning 19, 24, 34, 135-6; *see also* education; school contexts
Addison, M. 25
Adoption and Children Act 2002 **91**
adoptive families 2, 3, 82, *82*; *see also* family
adverse childhood experiences (ACEs): ACE strategies 39-40; alternative educational provisions and 135; attachment and 70-1; awareness 38-9, *38*; Bronfenbrenner's ecological systems and 79; Children Looked After (CLA) and 32; impact of 32-7, *33*, *35*; loving pedagogy and 40; neurodiversity and 49-52; origins of 29-31, *29*, *30*; overview i, vii, 28-9, 40-1, 49; statistics in the United Kingdom regarding 31-2; toxic stress and 48-9, *50*; training and *116*, 121, 135; *see also* trauma
aggression 35
Ainsworth, M. D. S. 59, 64, 65, 122
alcohol abuse 35
Allain, L. 16, 66
Anderson, E. 36
Anna Freud National Centre for Children and Families 47
anti-social behaviour 35
anxiety **23**, 35, 36, 58, 65
anxious attachment 59, 60-1, *61*, 63, 69; *see also* attachment
attachment: adverse childhood experiences (ACEs) and 38; anxious attachment 60-1, *61*, 63; attachment-aware schools 117-19; avoidant attachment 61-2, *62*, 64; Children Looked After (CLA) and 66-8; disorganized attachment 62-3, 64; internal working model and 64-5; loving pedagogy and 40; modern attachment theory 64-5; nurture as a strategy and 122-3; origins of attachment theory and 58-64, *60*, *61*, *62*; overview 57-8, 70-1; reactive attachment disorder (RAD) and 65-6; secure attachment 59, *60*, 63, 67-9; sibling relationships and 83; training and 132; trauma-informed practices and 70; "triangle of love" and 69; *see also* attachment theory; relationships
Attachment Aware Schools project 118-19, *119*
attachment theory: internal working model and 64-5; modern attachment theory 64-5; origins of 58-64, *60*, *61*, *62*; *see also* attachment
attention-deficit/hyperactivity disorder (ADHD) 44-5, *45*, 50-1, *52*; *see also* neurodiversity
Austin, A. 36
autism 44-5, *45*, 50-1, *52*; *see also* neurodiversity
avoidant attachment 59, 61-2, *62*, 64, 69; *see also* attachment

B
Baines, E. *119*, 120
Bandura, A. 22
Banerjee, R. 119, 124
Bartlett, S. 18
Bauman, Zygmunt 8-9
Becker, H. S. 18
Beckes, L. 61
behavioural symptoms 51, *85*; *see also* high risk behaviours
Bellis, M. A. 32
belonging, sense of 8-9, *12*
Bennion, K. 122
Berridge, D. 124, 132
Best, S. 9
bipolar disorder 44; *see also* neurodiversity
Biringen, Z. 59
birth family contact 85-7, *85*, *86*, *87*; *see also* family; sibling relationships

Birth to 5 Matters 90
Blodgett, C. 34
Boldt, L. 58
Bolton, G. 130
Bosmans, G. 65
Botha, M. 44
Bourdieu, Pierre 8
Bowlby, John 58, 59, 64, 65, 75, 122
Bradbury, A. 76, 77, 122, 132
brain development: impact of ACEs on 33-4, *33*, 49; nurture as a strategy and 122; overview 54-5; toxic stress and 48-9, *50*; *see also* developmental processes; neurodiversity; neurological development
Breeze, M. 25
Brighter Futures (2024) training and support 116-8, *116*, 132
Brock, T. 8, 18, 76
Bronfenbrenner, U. 76-8, 121
Bronfenbrenner's ecological systems 76-8, *76*
Brown, A. 8
Brown, E. C. 70
bullying *30*
Burton, D. 18

C
Cahill, O. 66
Cameron, C. 58, 121
care, experienced 20, 21, 60
care cliff 99
care leavers 90, 98, 99-100
care order 3
care planning 110
caregivers 58-64, *60*, *61*, *62*, 65-6
Carter, C. 8
case system *30*
case workers *see* social workers; superheroes
Cavanaugh, B. 70
child protection 95-99, *116*
childhood abuse *29*; *see also* abuse; adverse childhood experiences (ACEs)
Children (Leaving Care) Act 2000 **91**
Children Act 1989 2-3, 4-5, 85, **91**, 107, 109, 110, 123, 136
Children Act 2004 **91**
Children and Families Act 2014 17, **91**, 123
Children and Social Work Act 2017 **91**
Children in Care (CIC) *see* hildren Looked After (CLA)
Children Looked After (CLA): adverse childhood experiences (ACEs) and 32; alternative educational provisions and 135; attachment and 66-8, 70-1; birth family contact and 85-7, *85*, *86*, *87*; Bronfenbrenner's ecological systems and 76-8; care leavers and 90, 98, 99-100; challenges for professionals working with 112-3; family and 74, 77, 85-6, *85*, *86*; listening and responding to 136-8; living arrangements for 81-4, *82*, *83*, *84*; neurodiversity and 49-52; overview i, vi-vii, 2-5, *3*, 12-3, 89, 129-31, 137; perspectives of superheroes by 105-9, *105*, *107*; professional support and 134-5; reflective practice and 130-2; reform in public perception and 135-6, **136**; relationships and 67-9; sibling relationships and 85-6, *85*, *86*; terminology 16-7; Virtual Schools and 123-5
Children's Social Care National Framework 2023 96-99, 136
Children's Social Care Reforms 95-99, 133-4
Children's World Report 94
Clare, A. 68
Clarke, L. 36
Cocker, C. 16, 66
cognitive development *33*, 34, 54-5
cognitive functioning **23**, 45; *see also* neurodiversity
Collins, S. 66, 78
community 8-9, *30*, *107*, 111, 117
Conkbayir, M. 33, 34, 36, 122
Continuous Professional Development (CPD) 130, 131-3
Coram 111
Cortese, S. 50, 51
counsellers *see* professional support; superheroes
Coutts, N. 130
Crandall, A. 34
Crawford, S. 8
criminality 18, *35*
crisis 3, 4, 81-2
Crowley, K. 6
Cui, M. 84
cultural contexts 8, 9-10, 47, 85
Cumulative Risk Theory 33

D
Dansey, D. 17
Davidson, K. 6
Davis, T. 50
Day, A. 18, 24
death *30*, *33*
Delderfield, R. 130

delinquency 35
depression 29, 35, 36, 49
designated teacher **116**, 120; see also teachers
Devaney, J. 29
Development Matters 90
developmental processes: impact of ACEs on 33-7, *33, 35*, 49; neurodiversity and 49-50, 54-5; secure attachment and 59; sibling relationships and 84; see also brain development; neurological development
Dhakras, 2017 50
Dhakras, S. 51
diagnosis 51
Diaz, C. 137
disability: impact of ACEs and *33*, 36; models of 46-7; overview 44; parental illness or disability 3, 4; reasons a child may be taken into care 3; stigma and 24; see also neurodiversity
discrimination 23-4
disease *33*, 36
disorganized attachment 59, 62-3, 64, 69; see also attachment
divorce 29; see also adverse childhood experiences (ACEs)
doctors and GPs 111-2, *112*; see also professional support; superheroes
domestic violence 29; see also adverse childhood experiences (ACEs)
Dougherty, S. 24
Dozier, M. 58
Drew, H. 124
drug abuse 35
Du Paul, G. J. 63
Dunn, J. 22
Durkheim, E. 75-6, *75*
dyscalculia 45, *45*, 52; see also neurodiversity
dysgraphia *45*; see also neurodiversity
dyslexia 44-5, *45*, 51, 52; see also neurodiversity
dyspraxia 44-5, *45*, 51; see also neurodiversity

E
early education 92, 94-5, 133; see also education
Early Years Foundation Stage (EYFS) 90, 92-3, 131
Early Years Pupil Premium (EYPP) 92
eating disorders 35
Eaude, Tony 9-10
ecological systems approach 76-8, *76*

economic factors vi, 4, *30*, 75
education: adverse childhood experiences (ACEs) and 34; alternative provisions in 137; Brighter Futures (2024) training and support and 116-7, *116*; Children Looked After (CLA) and 90; Early Years Foundation Stage (EYFS) and 90, 92-3; inequalities in 134-5; list of legislation and **91**; National Curriculum and 90, 93-4, **93**; overview vi, 115-6; Pupil Premium and Pupil Premium Plus and 94-6, **95**; stigma and 25; Virtual Schools and 123-6; see also academic functioning; school contexts; teachers
Education and Inspection Act 2006 **91**
educational support staff 116-7, *116*; see also professional support; superheroes; teachers
Edwards, M. 75
Ellis, E. E. 65
emergency care teams see professional support; superheroes
emergency foster carers 81-3, *81*; see also family; foster families/placement
Emergency Protection Order of the Children Act (1989) 5; see also Children Act 1989
Emotion Coaching 119-21, *119*, 132
emotional abuse 29; see also abuse; adverse childhood experiences (ACEs)
emotional development: attachment-aware schools and 118; impact of ACEs and *33*, 34-5; neurodiversity and 54-5; serve and return interactions and 48; sibling relationships and 84
emotional factors 51, 75, 86
emotional intelligence 122
emotional neglect 29; see also adverse childhood experiences (ACEs)
empathy 40, 119-20, *119*, 122
environment *30*, 38-9, *38*, 54-5
Erikson, Erik 6-8, **7**
esteem needs 12
ethnicity 24
Evans, A. 34
Evans, R. 95
expanded ACEs *30*; see also adverse childhood experiences (ACEs)
expectations 8-9, 22, 118
extended family 78, *78*; see also family

F
facilitator **116**, 125; see also teachers
family: birth family contact and 85-7, *85, 86, 87*; family relationships for CLA

83–5, *83*, *84*, *87*; importance of 76–8, *76*; living arrangements for CLA 79–82, *80*, *81*, *83*; National Framework 2023 and 97–99; overview 74–6, *75*, 78–81, *79*, *80*, 89–90; perspectives of CLA and *109*, *110*; reasons a child may be taken into care 3, 4; sibling relationships 85–6, *85*, *86*, 89; *see also* adoptive families; adverse childhood experiences (ACEs); foster families/placement
Faraone, S. 47
Farr, W. 119
Felitti, V. J. 29, 120
Ferguson, H. 131
Fieller, D. 16, 25–6
financial factors *see* economic factors
Fisher, H. 32
flight or fight response *38*, 39, 65
following instructions 34
Fond, M. 33
foster families/placement: birth family contact and 85–7, *86*, *87*; family and 74; foster carers 110–1; language and 25–6; overview 2, 79–80, *80*, 108; sibling relationships and 83–4; *see also* Children Looked After (CLA); family; superheroes
Fouts, H. N. 6
Francis, Y. 122
Frederick, J. 29
freeze response 38–9, *38*, 65
friendships 78; *see also* peer relationships
functionalism 75–6, *75*
funding 94–5, **95**, 100

G
Gao, W. 32
Garrido, E. F. 35
Gelman, S. 47
genetic factors 47
Gibson, M. 130
Giddens, S. 118
Gilbert, L. 119
Gillath, O. 65
Gilmore, J. H. 32
Goffin, K. 58
Goffman, E. 23–4
Golding, K. 24
Goleman, D. 122
Golmakani, N. 57
Goodall, K. 65
Gorard, S. 94
Gottman, J. M. 119, 120
government views 100–1; *see also* guidance; legislation; policy; procedure
Grimmer, T. 40, 68, 69, 76, 77, 122, 133
guidance 89, **90**, 100–1, 119–20, *119*, 132

H
habitus 8
Hadon, A. 33
Hammond, S. 134
Hanson, K. 131
Hardcastle, K. 34
Hargreaves, D. 18
Harris, T. 22
Harvey, J. 108, 109
Heady, N. 50, 51
health 3, 4, 36, 111
health professionals 111–2, *112*; *see also* professional support; superheroes
Hendry, E. 99
Hierarchy of Needs 11–2, *12*, 59
high risk behaviours 33, 35–6, *35*; *see also* behavioural symptoms
Hill, M. 30
Hirst, M. 58, 69
Holmes, J. 66
Holt, S. 66
Hooven, C. 119
Horsburgh, J. 16
Howe, D. 64
Huat See, B. 94
Hughes, A. 65, 69, 109
Hughes, D. 39–40
Hull, L. 51
Humrich, S. 122

I
identity: adverse childhood experiences (ACEs) and 28; Bauman's notion of liquidity modernity 8–9; birth family contact and 85; Bourdieu's theory 8; Eaude's concept of culture and 9–10; Erikson's psychosocial theory 6–8, **7**; labelling and 17–8; needs of children and 11–2, *12*; overview vi, 6–8, **7**, 12–3; peer relationships and 78
illness 3, 4, 111
income *see* financial factors
independence 58, 59
Initial Teacher Training Core Content Framework 117–19
insecure attachment 65–6, 69; *see also* anxious attachment; attachment; avoidant attachment; disorganized attachment
interactions between children and adults: attachment and 58–64, *60*, *61*, *62*, 68–9, 70; overview 48–9, *50*; trauma-informed practices and 70
interests 52–3, *52*
internal working model 64–5; *see also* attachment
Ireland, L. 108, 109

J
Jobs, Steve **136**
John, M. 17
Jones, 2017 36

K
Kaip, D. 108, 109
Karantzas, G. 65
Karatekin, C. *30*
Katz, C. 65
Katz, L. F. 119
Kelly, P. 118
Kendall-Taylor, N. 33
Keoghan, Barry 135, **136**
kinship care 2, 74, 98, 123
kinship families 79, *79*; see also family
Kirwan, G. 66
Knickmeyer, R. C. 32
Kobak, R. 65
Kochanska, G. 58
Krawczyk, K. M. 120

L
labelling i, vii, 15, 16, 17-23, **20**, **23**; neurodiversity and 51
language 15, 25-6, 134; see also terminology
Lanigan, J. D. 34
laws *see* legislation
Leaf Complex Care 52
learning 34, 40, *116*, 117
leaving care 90, 98, 99-101
Leckenby, N. 32
Lee-Brindle, G. F. 78
Legg, H. 51
legislation 89, 90, **90, 91**
Lewis, M. 25
LGBTQ+ 24
liquid modernity 8-9
Looked After hildren (LAC) 16; see also Children Looked After (CLA)
loss *30*, 85
Loughlin, M. 16, 25-6
love and belonging needs 8-9, *12*
loving pedagogy 40
Lowey, H. 32
Luke, I. 22
Lyu, X. 61

M
Macblain, S. 22
Macer, M. 96, 97, 132
Mackin, J. 62-3
Maguire, T. 58
Mandy, W. 51
Mannay, D. 19

Marcia, J. E. 6
marginalisation 24
Maslow, A. H. 12
Maslow's Hierarchy of Needs 11-2, *12*, 59
Mathers, S. 92
Maynard, B. R. 70
McArdle, K. 130
McAuley, C. 50
McBlain, S. 59
McGuire-Snieckus, R. 120
McWey, L. M. 84
Meakings, S. 17
medical model of disability 47; see also disability; neurodiversity
Menedez, D. 47
mental development 48
mental health/illness 29, 36, 55, 120; see also adverse childhood experiences (ACEs)
Merton, R. 22
microsystem 77
Miller, S. 130
Minett, P. 122
misophonia 45; see also neurodiversity
models of disability 46-7; see also disability; neurodiversity
modernity 8-9
Monroe, Marilyn **136**
Moon, J. A. 132
Morrisey, Neil **136**
Morton, Samantha **136**
motivational factors **23**
Murphy, C. 99
Murphy, Eddie **136**
Murphy, R. 65
Murray, R. 32

N
Naish, S. 12, 80
National Curriculum 90, 93-4, **93**
National Framework 2023 96-9
National Society for the Prevention of Cruelty to Children 2024 98-9
Neaum, S. 58
needs of children 11-2, *12*, 59, 83-5
neglect 3, 4, *29*; see also adverse childhood experiences (ACEs)
neurodevelopment 33-4, *33*, 43-4
neurodivergent **44**
neurodiversity: adverse childhood experiences (ACEs) and 49-52; Children Looked After (CLA) and 49-52; inequalities in education and 134-5; informed model 47; models of disability and 46-7; organisations and services to support CLA 54, **54**; overview 43-6,

44, 45, 54-5; positive aspects of 52-3, 53; strategies for neurodiverse children 52; toxic stress and 48-9, 50; *see also* disability
neurological development 33-4, 33; *see also* brain development; developmental processes
neuroscience 43, 50
neurotypical **44**
Newman-Taylor, K. 58
nuclear family 78-9, 79; *see also* family
nurses *see* professional support; superheroes
nurture as a strategy 122-3
Nutbrown, K. 68

O
O'Connor, A. 59
Ofsted 93-4, 125, 137
Ogundele, M. 50
organisations and services to support CLA 54, **54**
Owen, C. 24

P
PACE approach (**P**layfulness, **A**cceptance, **C**uriosity, and **E**mpathy) 39-40
Page, J. 40, 68, 69
Pallini, S. 61, 63
parent anti-social behaviour 3, 4
parental illness or disability 3, 4; *see also* disability; illness
parental incarceration 29; *see also* adverse childhood experiences (ACEs)
Parfitt, A. 94, 95, 132
Parsons, S. 50
Partridge, O. 58
peer relationships 16-7, 30, 78, 116; *see also* relationships
Personal Education Plan (PEP) 92, 124-5
person-centered approach 26
physical abuse 29; *see also* abuse; adverse childhood experiences (ACEs)
physical health 3, 4, 36, 111
physical neglect 29; *see also* adverse childhood experiences (ACEs); neglect
physiological needs 11-2, 12
Pinto, C. 51
placement 3, 74, 84, 97-99, 113; *see also* foster families/placement; kinship care
placement order 3, 82
playfulness 39, 121-3
police officers 109; *see also* professional support; superheroes
policy 89, **90**, 100-1, 119
polyvagal theory 38-9, 38

Porges, Stephen 38-9, 38
poverty 30; *see also* economic factors
primary school education 95-6, **95**, 135; *see also* education
procedure **90**
professional love 40
professional support: attachment and 69; birth family contact and 85-7, 87; Bronfenbrenner's ecological systems and 77-8; challenges for professionals working with CLA 112-3; Continuous Professional Development (CPD) and 132; high risk behaviours and 36; need for 131-2; neurodiversity 51; nurture as a strategy and 122-3; perspectives of CLA and 105-9, 105, 107; professional love 40; reflective practice and 130-2; roles and responsibilities of 109-112, 112, 134-5; sibling relationships and 83-4, 84; Theraplay project 121-2; training and development and 132; trauma-informed practices and 70; *see also* superheroes
Promoting the Education of Looked-After Children and Previously Looked-After Children 93
psychosocial theory of identity formation 6-8, **7**; *see also* identity
public perception reform 135-7, **136**
Pupil Premium Plus (PPP) 94-5, **95**, 124-5, 132
Pupil Premium (PP) 94-5, **95**

R
Raby, K. L. 58
Rahilly, T. 10
Raud, R. 8-9
reactive attachment disorder (RAD) 65-6
Read, S. 94, 95, 132
reasons a child may be taken into care 2-5, 3
Reay, D. 6
Rees, C. 58, 60
reflective practice 130-2
Reimer, D. 58, 121
relationships: adverse childhood experiences (ACEs) and 35, 38; attachment theory and 58; birth family contact 87-9, 87, 88, 89; Brighter Futures (2024) training and support and 116; Bronfenbrenner's ecological systems and 76-8; Children Looked After (CLA) and 67-9; Internet and 44; labelling and 18; loving pedagogy and 40; overview i, 16-7; sibling relationships 85-6, 85, 86, 89; strategies for developing secure

attachment 67-9; "triangle of love" and 69; see also attachment; family
religious backgrounds 24
residential care 2, 51
respite foster carers 82-3, *83*; see also family; foster families/placement
restorative approaches *116*
risk of harm *3*, 4-5, 98, 110
Roberts, C. 24
Roberts, L. 24
role models 34-5
Rollins, E. M. 34
Romney, A. *119*, 120
Rose, J. 120, 121
Rutter, M. 33

S
Saadabadi, A. 65
safety: attachment and 59; family and 75; needs of children 11-2, *12*; polyvagal theory and 38-9, *38*; trust and 108; unsafe environments 30
Sambell, K. 130
Savage, E. 62
Schön, D. 131
school contexts: attachment-aware schools 117-9; Brighter Futures (2024) training and support and 116-7, *116*; Bronfenbrenner's ecological systems and 77-8; emotion coaching and 119-21, *119*; impact of ACEs and 34; labelling and 18-9; nurture as a strategy and 122-3; overview 115-6, 126; stigma and 25; Theraplay project and 121-2; trauma-informed schools and 120-1; Virtual Schools and 123-6; see also academic functioning; education; teachers
Scott, K. 29
Sebba, J. 123, 124, 132
secondary school education 93-4, **93**, 135; see also education
secure attachment 59, *60*, 63, 67-9; see also attachment
security *12*, 29, 40, 58-9, 60, 69, 133
self-actualisation *12*
self-awareness 122
self-confidence 36
self-efficacy 22-3, **23**
self-esteem 36, 55
self-fulfilling prophecy 22; see also labelling
self-harm 35
self-regulation 34-5, 58, 122
self-reliance 67
Selwyn, J. 17
sense of community 111, 117; see also community

separation, family 30, 85-6; see also family
serve and return interactions 48
service provision 51; see also professional support
sexual abuse *29*; see also abuse; adverse childhood experiences (ACEs)
sexual behaviour 35
Shbero, D. 17
sibling relationships 83-6, *84*, *86*, *89*; see also birth family contact; family
Siddiqui, N. 94
Silver, M. 24
Singer 44
single-parent family 79, *79*; see also family
skills 52-3, *52*
Skinner, E. 65
slow processing speed *45*; see also neurodiversity
Smith, M. 58, 121
Smith, P. 76
social development: impact of ACEs and *33*, 34-5; serve and return interactions and 48; sibling relationships and 83
social factors: disability and 47; family and 75-6, *75*; identity and 8-9; impact of ACEs and 36, 51; Internet and 44; overview vi; stigma and 23-5
social model of disability 46-7; see also disability; neurodiversity
social services 2, 109-111; see also Children Looked After (CLA); professional support
social workers 77, 99, 109-111, 133-4; see also professional support; superheroes
socialisation 9-10, 75, 122
socioeconomic status 24; see also economic factors
solid modernity 9
Somerville, M. P. *119*, 120
Special Educational Needs and Disability (SEND) Code of Practice: 0 to 25 years 2015 97
Spratt, T. 29
Sroufe, A. 58
stammering *45*; see also neurodiversity
standards, educational 92, 95-6, **93**, 134-5
Statham, J. 24
stepfamilies 80, *80*; see also family
stereotyping 18, 23-4, 26
Stewart, D. 22
stigma: disability and 47; labelling and 18; language and 25-6; overview i, vii, 15, 23-5; reform in public perception and 137-8, **136**
Strand, P. S. 62
strengths 52-3, *53*

stress 35, 48-9, 50
substance abuse 29, 35; see also adverse childhood experiences (ACEs)
superheroes: challenges for professionals working with CLA 114-5; examples of 10; overview 103-5, 104, 113; perspectives of CLA and 105-9, 105, 10; roles and responsibilities of 109-13, 112; see also professional support; social workers; teachers
Swailes, R. 76
Szeintuch, S. 40

T
Taussig, H. N. 35
Taylor, Y. 2
Teacher Training Core Content Framework 134-5
teachers: attachment-aware schools and 119-21; Brighter Futures (2024) training and support and 118-9, 118; Bronfenbrenner's ecological systems and 77-8; emotion coaching and 121-2, 121; labelling and 18; National Curriculum and 93-5, 9; nurture as a strategy and 122-3; overview **116**, 126; roles and responsibilities of 109, 115-6; training and 116-18, 116, 125, 132-3; trauma-informed schools and 120-; Virtual Schools and 123-6; see also education; professional support; school contexts; superheroes
temporary crisis 4, 64
terminology: government views **92**; neurological terms 43-4, **44**, 45-6; overview 1-2, 12-3, 16-7, 17; see also language
therapists see professional support; superheroes
Theraplay project 123-4
Thomas, N. P. 77
threat 38-9, 38
Tickle, A. 51
Tourette's syndrome 45, 52; see also neurodiversity
toxic stress 48-9, 50; see also stress
traditional family 78-9, 79; see also family
training: Brighter Futures (2024) training and support and 118-9, 118; Continuous Professional Development (CPD) and 132; for early childhood practitioners 135; Initial Teacher Training Core Content Framework 119-20; overview 134; for social workers 135-6; for teachers 134-5
transitional support see care leavers
trauma: birth family contact and 87; impact of 33; neurodiversity and 49-50; relationships and 38; sibling relationships and 86; trauma-informed practices and 70; trauma-informed schools and 120-1; traumatic loss 30; see also adverse childhood experiences (ACEs)
"triangle of love" 69
Trivedi, G. 32
Trotta, A. 32
trust **7**, 78, 106, 109

U
unconditional love 39
United Nations Conventions of the Rights of the Child 6, 115, 116-7
unsafe environments see safety

V
Van Tieghem, M. 35
violence 30, 35-6, 35; see also aggression
Virtual Schools/Virtual School Head 94-5, **116**, 123-6, 132; see also teachers
Vossen, J. J. 62

W
Wardecker, B. M. 61
Warrington, C. 78
Watt, L. 118
Weare, K. 119
Webster, E. M. 32
Weiler, L. M. 35
well-being 118, 119, 122-3
Wellborn, J. 65
Wijedasa, D. 17
Willis, R. 50, 51
Winter, K. 77
Wojciak, A. S. 86
Woodrow, A. 65
Working Together to Safeguard Children 2023 97
workplace settings 25
worry 36
Wurster, H. 59

Y
Yilanli, M. 65
York, W. 36

For Product Safety Concerns and Information please contact our EU
representative GPSR@taylorandfrancis.com
Taylor & Francis Verlag GmbH, Kaufingerstraße 24, 80331 München, Germany

www.ingramcontent.com/pod-product-compliance
Lightning Source LLC
Chambersburg PA
CBHW060301240426
43661CB00060B/2857